Realism and Revolution

REALISM
AND
REVOLUTION

Balzac, Stendhal, Zola,
and the
Performances of History

SANDY PETREY

CORNELL UNIVERSITY PRESS
Ithaca and London

First published 1988 by Cornell University Press.

International Standard Book Number 0-8014-2216-7
Library of Congress Catalog Card Number 88-18117
Printed in the United States of America
*Librarians: Library of Congress cataloging information
appears on the last page of the book.*

*The paper in this book is acid-free and meets the guidelines for
permanence and durability of the Committee on Production Guidelines
for Book Longevity of the Council on Library Resources.*

For my parents

Contents

vii

Acknowledgments

The bulk of Chapter 2 appeared in *PMLA* 102 (1987). A significant portion of Chapter 4 appeared in *Neohelicon* 15 (1988). Parts of Chapter 5 were incorporated in articles that appeared in *Littérature*, no. 22 (May 1976), and *Europe*, no. 678 (October 1985). I am grateful to all four journals for permission to use this material here.

S. P.

Stony Brook, New York

Realism and Revolution

Realism is an issue not only for literature: it is a major political, philosophical and practical issue and must be handled and explained as such—as a matter of general human interest.

—Bertolt Brecht

Introduction:
The Baldness of the Present King
of France

Realism and Revolution addresses realist fiction as exemplified in the nineteenth-century French novel. My point of departure is the recent critical assault on the representational categories long identified with the achievements of realist prose; I argue that the dilemmas of representation, far from being realism's blind spot, figure among its major narrative subjects.

J. L. Austin's concept of speech acts furnishes my principal theoretical support. Austin's understanding of constative language relies on the same repudiation of direct reference that animates structuralist and poststructuralist criticism. Whereas recent literary theorists have taken language's freedom from any obligation to facts as the pretext for analyzing the infinite varieties of linguistic play, however, speech-act theory as I use it demands concomitant attention to the socially bound impact of linguistic work. While stressing the conventional nature of reality, Austin remains fully aware that reality as conventionally established is a dominant presence in human existence. *Realism and Revolution* defines the nineteenth-century French novel as displaying a comparably dual awareness that words freed from their referential ground are nonetheless susceptible to stern social regimentation.

I defend that definition through analysis of three recognized masterpieces of French realism. Although I make no attempt to survey realism comprehensively, my assumption is that *Le Père Goriot*, *Le Rouge et le noir*, and *Germinal* are sufficiently enshrined in the realist canon to underwrite generalization. Each analysis of an individual novel emphasizes the textual delineation of constative language as a verbal form deprived of objective referential identity and imbued with immense historical stature. Each also addresses the ways speech-act theory can partially reconcile the contradictory assessments of realism associated with traditional and contemporary criticism.

Confronting Austin with nineteenth-century French fiction and twentieth-century French theory entails a certain violence to the philosophical tradition through (and against) which Austin developed his ideas. If that tradition had a motto, it would almost certainly be "The present king of France is bald." Bertrand Russell discussed that sentence at length in his classic 1905 article "On Denoting," and it has subsequently become one of the most extensively analyzed propositions of the twentieth century. Russell's point is that, because a denoting phrase such as "the present king of France" has no referent, every proposition containing such a phrase as a primary constituent is necessarily false no matter what it says. Whereas we can readily determine the accuracy of a sentence such as "Telly Savalas is bald" by locating Telly Savalas and examining his head, we cannot locate the present king of France and therefore cannot truthfully assert that he is either bald or not bald.

The consequence is that fundamental principles of logic are not pertinent to propositions that denote a referent such as the present king of France. "By the law of excluded middle, either 'A is B' or 'A is not B' must be true. Hence either 'the present king of France is bald' or 'the present king of France is not bald' must be true. Yet if we enumerated the things that are bald, and then the things that are not bald, we should not find the present king of France in either list" (485). If the universe does not contain the entity designated by a given denoting phrase, that phrase invalidates every proposition in which it occurs.

But if the denoting phrase does have a referent, then propositions again become subject to the orderly rules of logic and truth. The problems presented by the present king of France disappear when (in 1905) Russell considers the present king of England. The reality of one king is nonproblematic, that of the other nonexistent. As a consequence, propositions about the two monarchs must be evaluated in distinct ways. What Russell calls "parity of form" is inapplicable apart from parity of reference.

The intriguing aspect of Russell's discussion of the kings of England and France (and of subsequent discussions of his discussion) is that one of the most historically contingent conditions imaginable, the status produced by a nation's form of government, appears in the guise of a given reality that need not be historically situated. Russell takes it for granted that there is an "actual man denoted" (483) by "the king of England" and that we could "enumerate" all the things existing in the universe without finding the king of France on the list. In "On Denoting," it matters not at all that there was in 1905 a group of people who could have readily told Russell whether the present king of France was bald by looking at the Bourbon pretender to the French throne, nor that there was in England a significantly more important group for whom "the king of England" was a string of nonsense syllables. Instead of collective action in concrete circumstances, denotation is for Russell an abstract exercise in formal logic.

> If "C" is a denoting phrase, say "the term having the property F," then
>   "C has the property ϕ" means "one and only one term has the property F, and that one has the property ϕ." If now the property F belongs to no terms, or to several, it follows that "C has the property ϕ" is false for *all* values of ϕ. Thus "the present king of France is bald" is certainly false. [490]

In that triumphant demonstration of what is "certainly false," Greek and Roman letters appear where description of social and historical conflict is needed.

Consider the situation of "the present king of France" at a period when social and historical conflict over the phrase's denoting power was at its most intense, the years of the French

3

Revolution. In early August of 1792, the sections of Paris declared that Louis XVI was not the present king of France. On the night of August 10, that declaration acquired overwhelming practical impact when the people invaded the Tuileries palace, massacred the king's guard and forced the royal family to seek the protection of the legislature. The remaining months of 1792 saw Louis XVI, king of France, become Louis Capet, citizen of France, a criminal put on trial and condemned to death for having acted as if he were a king. Between August 10, 1792, and Louis's execution on January 21, 1793, a physical referent continued to present such characteristics as a certain amount of hair that would permit classical evaluation of the truth value conveyed by descriptive statements about him. Furthermore, he remained the king of France for the immense majority of the world outside France and for a sizable portion of those his judges considered his fellow citizens. A statement along the lines of "the present king of France is on trial for his life" was thus simultaneously true and false, and the reasons for its ambiguity were not C, F, and φ but the ideological configuration of the community with which the person making the statement chose to be allied. For certain groups, the defendant was not a king but a traitor; for others, he was not a traitor but a king; for all, reference could not be assumed but had to be produced.

"On Denoting" addresses the difficulties denotation encounters when the referent does not exist. The situation of "the present king of France" between August 10, 1792, and January 21, 1793, introduces a radically different problem, that of a referent continuing to exist but no longer functioning as the object of reference. The problem continued after the execution of Louis XVI (or of Louis Capet). On January 21, 1793, did Louis's son become the present king of France? After the death of the son who both was and was not Louis XVII, was there immediately a present king of France named Louis XVIII? The answers to those questions were a matter not for semantic speculation but for sociopolitical commitment.

It is because the French Revolution presents this sort of problem of reference with such insistent constancy that *Realism and Revolution* begins its consideration of realism with a discussion of the Revolution, taken both as the historical precondition for the invention of realist prose and as a compelling demonstration of the concept of reference that prose articulates. The principal subject of the first chapter is not, however, the collective annihilation of the denotational value of "the present king of France" but collective institution of the denotational value of "National Assembly." In both the events of the Revolution and the texts of realist fiction, representation of a referent depends on social adherence without becoming in any way less solid than Russell takes unproblematically denoting phrases to be. In the circumstances prevailing in 1905, Russell and his readers were correct to assume that there was in fact a person denoted by "the present king of England," for the acquiescence of Edward VII's subjects sufficed to establish his royalty. Whether "king of England" and "king of France" have a referent is a matter not of abstract Being but of collective action. If collective action is efficacious, however, it produces a concrete entity that makes the phrase denoting it fully operational.

When Louis XVI became Louis Capet, he demonstrated that existence could be irrelevant to reference. When the Third Estate became the National Assembly, it made the same demonstration from the opposite direction, for here collective action suddenly produced the referent designated by a denoting phrase that was previously as vacuous as (to take one of Russell's examples) "the even prime other than 2." On June 16, 1789, there was no National Assembly of France. On June 17, 1789, the National Assembly was France's supreme governing body for a significant portion of the French population, a feat of denotational production that is a striking illustration of referential value proceeding from a collectivity to a phrase rather than, as Russell assumes, from an object to a name.

In other terms, the French Revolution was a period when verbal reference was at one and the same time distressingly contingent and comfortably reliable, and one of this book's principal arguments is that realist prose adopts an identical stance of simultaneous denial and affirmation of the referent's reality. In recent years, much of the most stimulating and influential criticism of French realism has concentrated on those components of classic realist texts that deny the validity of the referential claims previously made for the genre, claims formerly equated with the realist enterprise in its entirety. Epistemologically as well as etymologically, realism can be understood to depend on a positivist concept of the real, on the assumption that there is a precise, definable world in which entities straightforwardly present characteristics such as baldness or hairiness that can be examined to assess the accuracy of statements made about them. Since it is just this concept that structuralist and poststructuralist research has most convincingly attacked, realism as a genre has at times seemed to present the archaic resonance of Ptolemaic astronomy as a science. The term may designate a coherent body of work, but the grounds for the coherence are axioms that no longer command assent.

Roland Barthes's *S/Z* is to my mind the most persuasive and interesting confrontation between contemporary continental scholarship and realist fiction. Barthes's analysis of Balzac's *Sarrasine* undermines the inherited definitions of realism's specificity one by one, and it consequently serves as a starting point for the defense of realist specificity in my chapters on *Le Père Goriot*, *Le Rouge et le noir*, and *Germinal*. My contention in the chapter on *S/Z* is that, though each of Barthes's attacks on realist reference to reality is convincing, he neglects the ways Balzac's prose delineates the effect of a collective will toward validating the referent that same prose denounces as spurious. The chapters that follow the discussion of Barthes accept his major points as proven but still seek to define what can nevertheless be said about the realist accomplishment.

In Barthes's *S/Z*, denotation is a hopeless delusion. In Russell's "On Denoting," it is a rigorously reliable operation provided that what is denoted cooperates by existing. My argument is that realism incorporates aspects of both these contradictory positions by representing the referent as a reality produced by communal agreement to act *as if* denotation were feasible. For Barthes, both "the present king of France" and "the present king of England" are strings of signifiers that can never be extracted from the linguistic system in which they figure and can never be applied to the material facts of the nonlinguistic universe. For Russell, the two denoting phrases are absolutely distinct because one does in fact refer to the nonlinguistic universe and the other does not. For realist fiction, the two phrases are in themselves what Barthes sees but are in society what Russell sees. They are simultaneously separated from a referent by the abyss dividing distinct forms of being and susceptible to becoming referentially unimpeachable by the decision of the people of England or France that they will recognize their king. In realist fiction, the referent as classically defined is absent while the authority of the referent as classically extolled is omnipresent.

Austin's terminology is ideally suited to conveying realist articulation of the referent. What Austin calls constative language communicates with all the solidly grounded power attributed by Russell to the existence of a real, factual universe subject to accurate representation in linguistic propositions. Yet Austin situates the power of the constative not in a reified universe of facts but in the sociohistorically variable conventions recognized by those for whom the constative is factual. Austin is equally resolute in defining language as a performance rather than a description and in asserting that a performance taken to describe effectively does so. The allusion to Austin in my subtitle, *Balzac, Stendhal, Zola, and the Performances of History*, is an implicit contention that the speech-act vision of how the constative performs in a social formation provides a way to discuss Balzac, Stendhal, Zola, and the reality of history without repeating the errors that continental scholarship has persuasively condemned in considering prestructuralist understandings of the realist project.

This use of Austin to help find a way to avoid both the errors continental philosophy condemns and those it commits has an important precedent in recent use of the other major figure in Anglo-American philosophy of language, Ludwig Wittgenstein. Wittgenstein's concept of language games is very much in harmony with the exuberant celebration of ludic signs so prominent among recent French theorists. But the Wittgenstein of *Philosophical Investigations* was fully conscious that language games could not be considered in and of themselves: "What has to be accepted, the given, is—so one could say—*forms of life*" (226). Christopher Prendergast's *The Order of Mimesis* is thoroughly convincing on the affinities and distinctions between Wittgenstein and partisans of unlimited semiosis.

> What is known, or knowable, through language is what is constituted as known, and knowable, by a community of speakers who are, at once and indissociably, players of a language game and participants in a form of life. This approach has features in common with certain aspects of semiological thought . . . The critical difference, however, is that Wittgenstein avoids the potential idealist implications of this view by his insistence upon language as a medium of social practice; in the famous emphasis, to know a language is to participate in a form of life as a set of practical activities. [73]

That is why Wittgenstein contends that we could not understand a lion even if one could speak (223) and why the collapse of realist tenets detailed in *S/Z* does not prevent *Sarrasine* from maintaining a realist identity. A large number of realist texts could be quoted in support of Wittgenstein's position that games and social life are coextensive rather than mutually exclusive. Stendhal's comparison of existence in society to a game of whist in *La Chartreuse de Parme* is too well known to require another invocation. Take instead this insight by a character in one of Balzac's lesser-known works, *Le Contrat de mariage*. "I must play the game according to the rules of the society in which I am forced to live" (534; my translation). For Balzac as for Wittgenstein, what has to be accepted is that forms of life are a reality despite the fact that they are also a game.

Terry Eagleton's essay "Wittgenstein's Friends" orchestrates the same kind of confrontation between Wittgenstein and continental philosophy as Prendergast's *Order of Mimesis*. Although Eagleton is careful to insist that Wittgenstein must himself be supplemented by more historically minded thinkers such as Mikhail Bakhtin and Antonio Gramsci, he joins Prendergast in welcoming Wittgenstein's recognition that certain forms of life arrest the infinite uncertainty inherent in certain forms of thought. "What will determine whether we need to give another explanation is the social context in which we are arguing. Whether this explanation is found exact or desperately indeterminate depends on what we are doing. 'Doubting has an end,' Wittgenstein writes" (105). Like the referent, truth is not found but produced.

Eagleton and Prendergast both accord special importance to the parenthetical comment in Number 29 of Wittgenstein's *Philosophical Investigations*. "Do not say: 'There isn't a "last" definition.' That is just as if you chose to say: 'There isn't a last house in this road; one can always build another one' " (12). Of course one *can* always build another one, but at a given moment one house is last, one explanation functions as valid, there is a present king of England and there is not a present king of France. French realism too is concerned with representing simultaneously why no definition can be last in absolute terms and why some definition is last in social practice.

Despite their comparable stature in a single philosophical tradition, Austin and Wittgenstein are separated by a number of fundamental concepts and attitudes. The purpose of appealing to Wittgenstein in this introduction to my appropriation of Austin for reading French realist novels is not to assert an identity but to establish a precedent for the highly selective use I make of Austin. It is with reason that many of the same quotations from Wittgenstein appear in Prendergast, Eagleton, and other critics comparably concerned with the potential dialogue between continental and Anglo-American thought. Those critics' interest is stimulated by one current of a work flowing in many directions, and their choice of which aspects of Wittgenstein to include is informed by awareness that what they are excluding could underwrite significantly different conclusions.

I adopt the same stance toward Austin, whose penchant for contesting and refuting the points he makes is among his most memorable characteristics. Few thinkers have been more addicted to advancing and withdrawing theses, confronting arguments with counterarguments, basing crucial developments on grounds shown to be unreliable. To take the most pointed example, my use of Austin to discuss French realism will be based primarily on the fact that he collapses the distinction between constative and performative speech, between words that state a fact and words that accomplish a deed. But it must not be forgotten that the collapsed distinction between constative and performative originates and militates in Austin's own work, which endlessly interrogates everything it asserts. My appeals to the authority of Austin almost always put me in the uncomfortable position of simultaneously mounting covert challenges to that very authority.

Whether they celebrate or lament it, Austin's most interesting commentators have unanimously affirmed the extent of his penchant for undermining the categories he establishes. Let Jacques Derrida's "Signature Event Context" and Shoshana Felman's *Literary Speech Act* represent those writings that have vigorously applauded the self-contradictions in the founding documents of speech-act theory. For Derrida, Austin's analysis is "open, aporetic, in constant transformation, often more fruitful in the recognition of its impasses than in its positions" (322). Felman foregrounds the aporia and impasses by taking Austin's dissolution of oppositions as his major purpose in formulating them: "The Austinian analysis, if it is an act, is only the act of *failing to grasp the constative of the performative.* How, indeed, might one find the truth of that which, as such, deconstructs the criterion of truth itself? Austin's distinction ends up subverting itself; Austin abandons the statement/performance opposition in favor of a generalized theory of the performative. ... Austin takes into account the subversive, and self-subversive, potential of the performative" (63–64).

Felman's concept of subversion's self-subversion is strikingly apposite to the characteristic Austinian sequence of first asserting an opposition, then deconstructing it, then reintroducing it as preparation for its subsequent denial and reintroduction. The subversion of subversion is *orthodoxy*, and Austin's gleeful upsurges against philosophical stability are at times not far removed from staid arguments that philosophy should at least stabilize itself.

Among Anglo-American scholars who have worked through Austin's theory, John Searle occupies a special place. His book

Speech Acts remains an essential development of Austinian concepts, and Searle's polemic with Derrida starkly enacts the distinction between continental and American reaction to what Austin did with words. In his first contribution to that polemic, "Reiterating the Differences," Searle is constrained simultaneously to defend Austin against Derrida's reading and to distance his defense from the theory that is its supposed object: "I hold no brief for the details of Austin's theory of speech acts" (204). Austinian self-subversion is so infectious that Searle begins what was to become one of the best-known expositions of Austin's thought by distancing himself from Austin's thought.

Searle's difficulties with Austin are a continual theme in his elaborations of speech-act theory. For instance, the article entitled "A Classification of Illocutionary Acts" twice expresses the same exasperation at Austin's failure to see what Searle considers "plainly" self-evident. "Austin sometimes talks as if all performatives (and in the general theory, all illocutionary acts) required an extra-linguistic institution, but this is plainly not the case" (15). "Austin sometimes talks as if he thought all illocutionary acts were like this [requiring an extralinguistic institution], but plainly they are not" (6). For the purposes of this book, what is "plainly" the case is that neat separations between linguistic and extralinguistic entities are alien both to realist fiction and to the way "Austin sometimes talks." That he talks other ways at other times is of interest but not of moment.

These instances—and there are almost as many as there are commentators on speech acts—of reader response to the twists and turns in Austin's writing are quoted to make more palatable the fact that the following readings allude extensively to one part of a philosophical corpus without systematically addressing the other parts. If it is true that Austin says much that challenges my idea of the realist constative, it is also true that he says much to support it. Although my use of Austin is in all senses of the word *partial*, it is some comfort to reflect that the only Austinian who could be legitimately considered comprehensive is J. L. Austin.

The contradictory assessments of Austin made by Felman and

Searle, the former's celebrating the refusal to talk the same way at all times which is criticized by the latter, are closely connected to their different understandings of Austin's constative. Where Felman sees the performative nature of the constative as a feature that "deconstructs the criterion of truth," Searle defines the constative as expressing truth in its classic epistemological form. He distinguishes "brute facts" from "institutional facts" and illustrates the former by the force of gravitational attraction and the latter by a marriage. In this pair, institutional facts "are indeed facts; but their existence, unlike the existence of brute facts, presupposes the existence of certain human institutions. It is only given the institution of marriage that certain forms of behavior constitute Mr. Smith's marrying Miss Jones" (*Speech Acts*, 51). One of Searle's goals here is to furnish another refutation of Austin's implications that all speech acts require extralinguistic institutions. While affirming the importance of institutional stature for one class of facts, Searle preserves the traditional concept of the referent as the sole ground needed for brute facts to be brutally factual.

For Searle, the classical referent squarely explains the speech act performed by a referring expression.

> There are two generally recognized axioms concerning referring and referring expressions. As a rough formulation we might state them as follows.
>   1. Whatever is referred to must exist.
> Let us call this the axiom of existence.
>   2. If a predicate is true of an object it is true of anything identical with that object regardless of what expressions are used to refer to that object.
> Let us call this the axiom of identity. [*Speech Acts*, 77]

The same vision of speech acts that Felman saw as dispersing all the generally recognized axioms of verbal truth is for Searle fully complicitous with those axioms in their most unhedged formulation. As a result, Searle considers whether the present king of France is bald with the same conviction that there is simply no such person as Bertrand Russell (*Speech Acts*, 157–

62). The "axiom of existence" remains primordial even though the axiom of performance is on its trail.

Although I disagree with Searle's preservation of classic referential precepts, it remains crucial to my argument that he can without violence assimilate those precepts to Austin's work. The reason is again that speech-act theory leaves the *authority* of the referent intact even though it provides a way to transcend the question of the referent's *reality*. Searle simply attends to the fact that constative representation is simultaneously conventional and forceful, just as much reality as artifice. First brought forth to name representation of what words do not do, the constative retains something of its original character even when brought wholly under the aegis of words' doing. In order to conceive the constative, it is necessary to think of the reality it expresses as being both a product of human conventions and a supreme fact of human existence.

Austin does not eliminate or malign the referent but situates it elsewhere. The reality spoken in language, the things done by words, are for Austin no less powerful for their inability to escape their conventional linguistic matrix. The characteristic gesture of much continental thought is first to demonstrate language's liberation from the referent and then to consider the problem of the referent no longer urgent. Austin accepts the demonstration but rejects the consequence drawn from it. In speech-act theory, the act stays active despite its identification as speech. The referent, pitilessly barred from a world prior to language, keeps all its force as a component and consequence of language.

Even though he makes the point during his challenge to Austin in "Signature Event Context," Derrida cogently defines the dialectic of the referent characteristic of speech-act theory: "The performative's referent (although the word is inappropriate here, no doubt, such is the interest of Austin's finding) is not outside it, or in any case preceding it or before it. It does not describe something which exists outside and before language. It produces or transforms a situation, it operates" (321). Austin's exemplary contribution is a body of writings for which the word *referent* is at one and the same time no doubt inappropriate and absolutely unavoidable. Derrida must both use the word and deny its pertinence because he is addressing a thinker who is indifferent to the referent in itself yet uniquely sensitive to the referents in language.

The ambiguities of Austin's terminology are thus inherent in the scope of his ideas. In direct opposition to those among his fellow analytic philosophers concerned only with the correspondence between a linguistic proposition and the reality of the world, Austin focuses squarely on the reality effected by linguistic propositions. In contrast to those continental philosophers unconcerned with the distinctions among linguistic propositions, Austin shows that words do vastly different things depending on their relationship to the conventions through which their users coexist. Like realist fiction, speech-act theory takes words' inescapable conventionality not as reality's dismemberment but as its precondition.

Austin considers whether the present king of France is bald in Lecture XI of *How to Do Things with Words*, where he seems at first to accept unequivocally the same axioms of existence as Russell and Searle. But Lecture XI is the place where Austin makes his most influential criticisms of the concept of truth to which uninterrogated axioms of existence lead. The context of his remarks on Russell's bald king is therefore a demonstration that truth and falsity are not at all the simple matter of logic that Russell categorized as C, F, and φ. Austin: "In real life, as opposed to the simple situations envisaged in logical theory, one cannot always answer in a simple manner whether it is true or false" (143).

Here is how the bald king of France appears in *How to Do Things with Words*.

We have already noticed the case of a putative statement *presupposing* (as it is called) the existence of that which it refers to; if no such thing exists, "the statement" is not about anything. Now some say that in these circumstances, if, for example, someone asserts that the present king of France is bald, "the question whether he is bald does not arise"; but it is better to say that the putative statement is null and void, exactly as when I say that I sell you something but it is not mine or (having been burnt) is not any longer in existence. Contracts often are void because the objects they are about do not exist, which involves a breakdown of reference. [137]

Existence, not simply an either/or matter, is comparable to a contract in which conventions of private property have the same impact as the presence or absence of being. The "breakdown of reference," like the success of reference, must be considered in the community where it occurs rather than in the vacuum of logical theory.

The realist novel was the invention of a nation that had for four decades alternately experienced the failure of reference by "the present king of France" and the success of reference by the same denoting phrase. The Revolution and Restoration were a militantly sustained proof that the king's existence was indeed the effect of a contract. When the contract was recognized as valid, "the present king of France is" was referentially impeccable. When the contract was declared null and void, the same proposition was false. The readings of realist fiction in *Realism and Revolution* argue that the characters of Balzac, Stendhal, and Zola manifest an interaction of existence and ideology, of being and conventions, to which the French Revolution gave world-historical expression.

Those readings accordingly begin with the Revolution itself, seen through a perspective furnished by J. L. Austin. A perspective, not *the* perspective. Austin's paragraph on the present king of France is typical in that it can legitimately be read as perpetuating as well as interrogating the tradition of analytic philosophy to which it alludes, and my use of Austin in the following pages is often subject to revocation by Austin himself. Like realism and revolution, speech-act theory is open to diverse and divergent interpretations. Let the defense of my interpretation be the uses to which the rest of this book puts it.

I

The Revolution Takes a Name

On the morning of May 6, 1789, the representatives of France's Third Estate assembled in the Salle des Menus Plaisirs at Versailles for the first working session of the Estates General. They hoped that the delegates of the clergy and aristocracy would meet with them in a joint session like the one held the day before, when the three estates came together in that same hall for opening speeches by Louis XVI, the finance minister Jacques Necker, and the Garde des Sceaux.

The first piece of business after those inaugural speeches was verification of delegates' credentials, an apparent formality that in fact raised issues of the greatest consequence. Prior to the Estates General's convocation at Versailles, the Third Estate had secured the right to send a number of delegates greater than the combined total of those accorded the first two estates. But the question of whether this numerical advantage would have practical consequences remained open. Voting in the Estates General had traditionally been by order, not by head. If that procedure remained in force, the relative number of delegates representing any one order would be meaningless. The other orders would always be able to unite and form a two-to-one majority. If voting was by head, the Third Estate would dominate proceedings. If by order, it would be an impotent minority. To apply the famous opening words of the abbé Sieyès's pamphlet, the Third Estate was nothing if the orders voted separately; it was everything if voting occurred in common. The decision on how to count votes was equivalent to determining what the vote would show.

Despite its importance, voting procedure was an open question when the Estates General convened; the king and his ministers had refrained from deciding the most momentous issue facing them. Their diffidence was responsible for the extraordinary significance attached to the formality of verifying delegates' credentials. In the absence of a clear principle, precedence would undoubtedly rule. Preliminary procedures would establish the format for all actions to follow. Common verification of credentials was an essential first step toward common deliberations and common votes. Separate verification confirmed the Estates General's division into separate orders.

The Third Estate spent May 6 alone in the Salle des Menus Plaisirs. The clergy and aristocracy, in lucid concern for their self-interest, had withdrawn to separate halls, where each was proceeding to examine its members' papers independently. Clearly, the Third Estate could not respond in kind. Its goal was to repudiate the principle of separation, and it would be ratifying that principle if it conducted any business at all in the absence of the other orders. The only possible tactic was to refrain from official activity of any kind while unofficially attempting to persuade clergy and aristocracy to convene jointly. The Third Estate's adoption of that tactic condemned it to a long period of formal stagnation and informal ferment. Their credentials still unverified, the delegates of the bourgeoisie began a vigorous campaign to prove that the delegates of the other orders were in the same situation.

The stalemate lasted several weeks, during which nobility and priesthood imperturbably continued to meet separately while the Third Estate repeated its insistence that separate meetings were illegitimate. Finally, on June 10, 1789, Sieyès moved that there be one final effort to persuade the missing orders to convene in joint session so as to proceed at last with proper verification of credentials. If that attempt failed, the motion continued, the delegates of the Third Estate would verify the credentials of all delegates to the Estates General, including those from the first two orders. Any delegate, of whatever rank, who failed to appear and submit appropriate documentation would be marked as missing. Joint sessions would be declared to have begun regardless of whether they were in fact joint.

The message was sent on June 12. A handful of priests responded by joining the bourgeoisie. The aristocracy remained unanimously aloof. The Third Estate nevertheless implemented its decision to verify all delegates' credentials, and its determination to do so led to what is canonically the first revolutionary act of the French Revolution. On June 17, 1789, after completing the verification process, the Third Estate constituted itself as France's National Assembly and gave itself sole authority to levy France's taxes.

Among the most striking features of historical commentary on the French Revolution is the virulent disagreement over the meaning of any given revolutionary event. All the more remarkable, therefore, is the near unanimity with which historians and contemporaries have concurred on the critical significance of the National Assembly's constitution of itself. For François Furet and Denis Richet, when the Third Estate declared that it was no longer the Third Estate and transmuted a thousand-year-old political system into an Old Regime, "the great revolutionary act was consummated" (1, 98; all translations in this chapter are my own). Jules Michelet defined the two words *National Assembly* as "this simple formula of Sieyès that contained the Revolution" (1, 209). In Germaine de Staël's view, Sieyès's simple formula not only contained but actually effected the Revolution: "Sieyès proposed that they constitute themselves purely and simply as the National Assembly of France . . . that decree passed, and that decree was the revolution itself" (1, 204).

Memoirs of the period are filled with comparable assessments. Here is how the duchesse de Gontaut, governess to France's royal family during the Bourbon Restoration, describes June 17. "We are now in 1789, at the time of the Estates General, the members of which instituted themselves as the National Assembly and declared themselves in possession of all powers. That is when we can date the *Revolution*" (90). The italics are the duchesse de Gontaut's. For this devoted partisan of the monarchy no less than for those committed to a radically different social order, for historians of the French Revolution no less than for those who lived it, the Salle des Menus Plaisirs at Versailles became the scene of a world-shattering act when those within it gave themselves a name they did not possess before.

To adopt the title of François Furet's influential work, *Penser la révolution française*, how should we "think" the awesome historical consequences attached to what might have remained nothing more than a trivial shift in political terminology? Why was the replacement of Third Estate by National Assembly "the revolution itself" instead of a futile lexical game without political impact? This was not, after all, the Third Estate's first try at saying that it was something other than the Third Estate. From the time of their assembly at Versailles, the bourgeois delegates had referred to themselves as "the Commons," and noble and clerical delegates had vigorously protested that this name had no official status. During one of the meetings where delegates from the three orders aired their differences, for example, "a delegate of the aristocracy observed that this resolution used the word *Commons* to designate the Third Estate; that this innovation in words could lead to an innovation in principles, if it had not already done so; that he must therefore object to the expression and assert his inability to consent to its presence in the resolution" (Buchez and Roux, I, 423). This sort of terminological squabble, reminiscent of faculty senate meetings and surviving only in exquisitely detailed historical records, makes it even more remarkable that *National Assembly* was not a comparable piece of trivia but a supreme moment in creation of the modern world. On June 17, 1789, the words that name reality became one of the acts that make reality.

As a prime example of words that do things, the name taken by the Third Estate clearly illustrates the category of performative speech developed in J. L. Austin's *How to Do Things with Words*. For Austin, language performs by virtue of its position in the sets of social protocols allowing the members of any given community to coexist successfully. The first condition for a successful performative, which Austin labeled Rule A.l, is that "there must exist an accepted conventional procedure having a certain conventional effect" (14). The words "I now pronounce you husband and wife" produce a married couple, the words "Divorce is hereby pronounced" dissolve one, only by virtue of the conventions through which our society establishes and regulates marriage. Apart from the institution, the words do not do things but simply make noise. Conversely, efficacious utterance of the words confirms the institution's solidity. Performative speech is by definition—in its essence—socially specific. Its power is inseparable from a precise collective vision of what counts as authority in which sets of circumstances.

France's collective vision of what counted as authority in which sets of circumstances crumbled when the Third Estate successfully declared that it was the National Assembly. The change of names was a world-historical event because bourgeois seizure of the right to name challenged all conventional definitions of what the bourgeoisie could do.

In discussing the variety of performatives that he calls declarations, John Searle suggests the magnitude of the stakes when rules for making declarations are broken. For Searle, all declarations

> involve an extra-linguistic institution, a system of constitutive rules in addition to the constitutive rules of language, in order that the declaration may be successfully performed. The mastery of those rules which constitutes linguistic competence by the speaker and hearer is not in general sufficient for the performance of a declaration. In addition, there must exist an extra-linguistic institution and the speaker and hearer must occupy special places within this institution. ["Classification of Illocutionary Acts," 14]

Before June 17, 1789, France's institutions imposed the position of hearer on the members of the Third Estate. When bourgeois delegates refused that postion to speak of themselves in unprecedented terms, they did nothing less than challenge the entire system of constitutive rules and extralinguistic institutions holding the monarchist regime together. Germaine de Staël could legitimately call Sieyès's decree "the revolution itself" because what the Revolution was to do was already implicit in the words it chose to announce that its work had begun.

Louis XVI and his partisans responded to the announcement by pretending that its authority did not come from a new source but from the same "system of constitutive rules" under which France had functioned for a thousand years. According to conservative reasoning, the only possible ground for the Third Estate's declarative power was the king's convocation of the Estates General and the subsequent confusion created when one of the estates, the bourgeoisie, deliberated in the space where the king had originally convened all three estates, the Salle des Menus Plaisirs. By this logic, decrees passed in the Salle des Menus Plaisirs spoke for the Estates General as a whole merely because the opening ceremonies gave that hall the status of a meeting place for the entire body. The confusion could be dissipated by the simple device of barring the newly formed National Assembly from the hall that was the Assembly's only justification for calling itself National. Accordingly, on June 20, 1789—a rainy Saturday in Versailles—the delegates arrived for their scheduled meeting to find the Salle des Menus Plaisirs barred to them by soldiers with fixed bayonets. Wandering aimlessly through the rain, the delegates found an open building, that reserved for tennis games at Versailles, and declared that they were in official session.

The proceedings of that session are legendary. In the Tennis Court Oath, the National Assembly declared that its proceedings were official regardless of where its members convened—even the pretense of royal sanction through use of royal space was eliminated—and vowed not to separate until they had written a constitution for the French nation. The language used to formulate the oath compellingly displays the descriptive value of Austin's performative and Searle's declarations.

> The National Assembly, considering that, because it is called to set the constitution of the kingdom, effect the regeneration of public order, and maintain the true principles of the monarchy, nothing can prevent it from continuing its deliberations in whatever place it is forced to install itself, and considering finally that everywhere its members convene, there is the National Assembly;
>
> Resolves that all members of this assembly will immediately take a solemn vow never to separate, and to assemble wherever circumstances dictate, until the constitution of the kingdom is

established and secured on solid foundations. [Buchez and Roux,
II, 3]

This motion takes the "Whereas...Be it resolved" form of a
standard parliamentary decree. Remarkably, however, the "Be
it resolved" clauses do nothing more than repeat the "Whereas"
clauses. Instead of taking note of a situation and determining
to act on it, the National Assembly takes note of a situation
and determines that it is indeed the situation. Because "nothing
can prevent it from continuing its deliberations in whatever
place it is forced to install itself," the Assembly vows "to as-
semble wherever circumstances dictate," thus swearing to do
what nothing can keep from being done. Whereas it is "called
to set the constitution of the kingdom," it therefore resolves to
meet "until the constitution of the kingdom is established." As
each vow reiterates what was first presented as a statement, so
each statement has the performative impact of a vow.

In Austin's formulation of Rule A.1, performative speech does
things only because there *already* exists an accepted conventional procedure having conventional effect. In Searle's discussion of declarations, that conventional effect requires the *prior*
existence of an extralinguistic institution. The extraordinary
feature of the National Assembly's Tennis Court session is that
it declares its own authority while at the same time justifying
its right to do so on the basis of the authority that it is in the
process of declaring. A conventional procedure is inaugurated
at the moment that its conventional effect is assumed. An extralinguistic institution comes into being through a linguistic
pronouncement that derives whatever force it possesses from
the assumption that the institution was already in power. Many
declarations incorporate a specific reference to an established
extralinguistic institution through such formulas as "By the authority vested in me by the laws of this state." In memorable
contrast, the Tennis Court proceedings took the form of a complete tautology. By the authority vested in it, the National Assembly declared that authority was vested in it.

The conservative response was to invoke the authority vested
in the king to deny that authority was vested in the Third Estate.

On June 23, 1789, Louis XVI once again convened a joint session of the three estates in the Salle des Menus Plaisirs, where he and his spokesman were to speak without interruption or response. The king's three statements were broken by formal readings of fifty separate royal decisions. The most inflammatory was the first, which announced that everything the Third Estate had done, including renaming itself the National Assembly, was without effect. To the National Assembly's declaration of its existence was opposed the king's declaration of its nonexistence. In the words read to the assembled orders by the royal spokesman, "the king has declared null the deliberations taken by the deputies of the order of the Third Estate, on the 17th of this month, as well as those that may have followed, for they are illegal and unconstitutional" (Buchez and Roux, II, 13). The bourgeois delegates had declared that they were the National Assembly, that their sessions were official whenever and wherever they convened, and that their charge was to give France a constitution. Louis XVI declared that they were the "deputies of the order of the Third Estate," that their sessions were valid only when and where he decided, and that France already had a constitution allowing him to judge the Third Estate's actions "unconstitutional." The first act of the French Revolution was a stark conflict of performative speech. Which set of directly contradictory linguistic expressions would have extralinguistic validity?

The answer was that the National Assembly's expressions were valid. The conclusion of Louis's June 23 speech was this (classically performative) command: "I order you, gentlemen, to disperse at once" (Buchez and Roux, II, 21). Instead of obeying, the National Assembly remained in the Salle des Menus Plaisirs and announced that it was in official session. The first speaker it heard was the comte de Mirabeau, who made the thoroughly Austinian point that the content of the king's decisions was immaterial; what counted was that no king possessed the authority to make and impose them. Even though many of the fifty royal decrees, such as those concerning taxes and *lettres de cachet*, were in harmony with the National Assembly's intentions, they remained unacceptable because they required recognizing the conventional procedures with conventional effects characteristic of the Old Regime. Mirabeau's rhetoric was typically forceful: " 'Gentlemen,' he exclaimed, 'I admit that what you have just heard could be the salvation of the kingdom, were it not that the acts of despotism are always dangerous' " (Buchez and Roux, II, 21). At issue was not what was said but who had the right to say it, not the words spoken but the power to speak them.

Mirabeau's colleagues repeatedly made the same point in a series of ringing denials that the king's language had extralinguistic force. As was his habit in the Revolution's early days, Sieyès found the perfect formula to state that the royal words had not worked. "Gentlemen," Sieyès announced to his colleagues, "you are today what you were yesterday" (Buchez and Roux, II, 25). The National Assembly spoke, and it was born. The king spoke, and it refused to die. The words that had created it remained in force, those that had dissolved it melted away. Antoine Barnave used a Searlian vocabulary to say so: "You have declared what you are; you have no need of a sanction. ... It is your right to persist in the title of *National Assembly*" (Buchez and Roux, II, 23–24). To persist in a title was simultaneously to persist in a revolution. Choice and utterance of words was transformation and renewal of the world.

Austin's category of performative speech articulates this sort of interconnection between words and the world in ways not possible through competing visions of representation and reference. In each of the three stages in the National Assembly's creation—June 17, June 20, June 23—the referent and its representation were a single entity. The referent existed purely and simply because it was represented, the representation's validity was indistinguishable from its utterance. Barnave's "you have declared what you are" is from this perspective essentially the same as the Tennis Court resolution. If the bourgeois delegates were the National Assembly on June 23 because they had declared themselves to be so on June 17, what were they when they made the original declaration? The answer can only be that they were already what they declared themselves, for only thus could their declaration be authoritative. The same point applies to Sieyès's "you are today what you were yesterday." The Assembly alone had said what it was the day before. The tautological sequence is endless. At no point was there a body to which a name was applied, for application of the name and institution of the body were always already a single act.

And that act was "the revolution itself" because collective pressure created the conditions necessary for it to take effect. The previous discussion has addressed the linguistic conflicts between the king and National Assembly with little attention to the extralinguistic circumstances responsible for the outcome of the conflicts. The omission was strategic, but it must be corrected. Each stage in the verbal wars that began the French Revolution assumed and relied on the massive presence of armed force for its articulation. The National Assembly could change its name only because the people of Versailles (with the people of Paris behind when not beside them) established the material conditions necessary for authentic declarative power to exist. The king could deny that a name change had taken place only because he commanded an army of French and foreign soldiers theoretically prepared to defend his performative prerogatives. When armed men with fixed bayonets blocked the bourgeois delegates from the Salle des Menus Plaisirs on June 20, a huge and rebellious throng escorted the delegates to the Jeu de Paume to ratify the resolutions passed there. The lexical opposition *National Assembly/Third Estate* was also a political conflict of vast proportions. It unfolded in the context of the troubles in Paris that culminated in the storming of the Bastille on July 14, and the king's inability to enforce obedience to his pronouncements of June 23 was the direct result of his and his advisers' fears that such events were imminent. The National Assembly survived its interdiction by the king because the French people were prepared to defend its self-perpetuation. The force responsible for the success of the bourgeois performative expression during the week of June 17–23 was the mass that took the Bastille on July 14 and executed J.-F. Foulon and L.-B.-F. Berthier on July 27. Verbal innovation united with the supremely nonverbal facts that a royal fortress crumbled and pikes paraded severed heads through the streets of France's capital.

Speech-act theorists' unique sensitivity to the unity of linguistic performance and extralinguistic circumstances has produced the body of thought best suited to defining the significance of the National Assembly's indivisible birth and baptism. At the same time, however, those theorists have often assumed a stasis in linguistic formulas and extralinguistic conditions, a stasis that precludes recognition of revolutionary performatives such as those that created the National Assembly. In discussing declarations, for instance, John Searle insists on their conformity to a situation existing before them. Declarations instantaneously conform to reality because reality is so structured that nonconformity is impossible. "It is the defining characteristic of this class [declarations] that the successful performance of one of its members brings about the correspondence between the propositional content and reality, successful performance guarantees that the propositional content corresponds to the world" ("A Classification of Illocutionary Acts," 13). The French Revolution reversed the order of Searle's last point. Instead of propositional content corresponding to the world, the world was brought to correspond to propositional content. The National Assembly could make declarations only if it was indeed the National Assembly, and acquiring the authority to be what it claimed required radically new rules for determining which propositions corresponded to the world.

In both turbulent and stable times, the factors that determine the success of performative speech depend on a set of conventions arbitrarily institutionalized by a given collectivity. But in turbulent times, the collectivity must fight to make its conventions prevail. Whether a particular group constituted the National Assembly or the delegates of the Third Estate was a lexical problem with such awesome political consequences that its resolution required the overthrow of everything that had previously determined the correlation between the French language's propositional content and the French nation's reality.

Reading the originating events of the French Revolution as a war between opposing performatives demonstrates that what Austin calls illocutionary force is never a given but always a collective creation. When collectivities are in conflict, illocutionary values conflict as well. Before the Revolution, the authority of the king's speech appeared to proceed from an eternally unalterable source, the divine power underlying the king's divine right. Nothing less than God Himself validated the pronouncements of the man who ruled according to His supreme plan. In 1789, that appearance no longer prevailed. Royal authority was recognized to be the simple effect of national acquiescence before it. Since nothing extraneous to itself produced a collectivity's conventions, the collectivity was free to change those conventions however it liked. Performative language became not a source of stability but the stakes of a struggle. The birth of a National Assembly was the death of a national ideology.

In a talk he gave for the bicentennial of the American Declaration of Independence and subsequently published in the Galilée edition of *Otobiographies*, Jacques Derrida makes the important point that founding performatives are always the birth as well as the death of a national ideology. In 1776, while Thomas Jefferson and his colleagues were refusing the divine right of George III, they were simultaneously asserting the divine right of the American people. By its appeals to Nature and to Nature's God, the Declaration of Independence deviously disguised its usurpation of the performative as a constative representation of eternal, natural laws. In Derrida's assessment, therefore, this "declaration" is not a special case of performative language but yet another instance of constative appeal to the ultimate authority of truth and value that is the Godhead. "[God] founds natural laws, and thereby founds the whole game of presenting performative utterances *as* constative utterances" (25). When Jefferson announced what the colonies "are and of right ought to be," he took language out of human control and based it on divinity's attributes. " 'Are and ought to be': the 'and' here articulates and conjoins two discursive modalities, what is and what should be, statement and prescription, fact and right. *And* is God. . . . For the Declaration to have a meaning *and* an effect, there must be a last instance. God is the name, the best name, for this last instance and this ultimate signature"

(27). As in "Signature Event Context," Derrida's strategy with Austin's categories is to show that the performative is not in fact an exception to the appeals to a divine logos implicit in ordinary representational speech. What seemed to be language that acted was nothing more than language that stated. "The question remains . . . Who signs all these authorizations to sign?" (31) For Derrida, the answer is not human action in history but God in His heaven.

France in 1789 was no less committed to an ultimate ground than the United States in 1776. Among the representatives of the Third Estate, invocation of God and natural law was as common as among the representatives of the American colonies, and a deconstructive orientation could undoubtedly find the same desire for constative comfort in all historical explosions of performative rebellion. What a deconstructive perspective would miss, however, are the gradations among rebels' willingness to recognize that words can do as well as say, that they can work the will of humans as well as repeat the sayings of gods. *National Assembly* became the Revolution itself only after the representatives of the Third Estate had tried desperately to deny that their speech was in actuality an act. Their diffidence is blatant in the names they originally devised for the institution they were creating. Sieyès first proposed that the legislature he wanted to establish be called the "Assembly of the Recognized and Verified Representatives of the French Nation" (Buchez and Roux, I, 443), a lengthy paraphrase for the principle of common verification of credentials. Jean-Joseph Mounier made the paraphrase even lengthier by suggesting the comic-opera "Legitimate Assembly of the Representatives of the Larger Portion of the Nation, Acting in the Absence of the Smaller Portion." I.-R.-G. Le Chapelier countered with "Legally Verified Representatives of the French Nation," A.-F. Galand with "Legitimate and Active Assembly of the Representatives of the French Nation" (Buchez and Roux, I, 455, 459). It was not until midnight on June 16 that Sieyès put an end to the debates by altering his original motion to propose the title that Germaine de Staël equated with the Revolution itself. In the language Sieyès pro-

posed for the resolution adopted on June 17, 1789, "the denomination of *National Assembly* alone befits the assembly in
the present state of things." (Buchez and Roux, 1, 470).

The conflict over what the delegates of the Third Estate would
be when they stopped calling themselves the delegates of the
Third Estate is fascinating on several levels. First, the sheer
grotesqueness of the early suggestions is an especially eloquent
demonstration of the importance of language in politics. I find
it impossible to imagine Parisian sans-culottes storming the Bastille while screaming not "Long live the National Assembly"
but "Long live the Legitimate Assembly of the Representatives
of the Larger Portion of the Nation, Acting in the Absence of
the Smaller Portion." The respiratory obstacles alone would
have been insurmountable.

Moreover, the twenty words and one comma in Mounier's
proposal have an ideologically defensive character ill suited to
the ideological assault that the bourgeois delegates were making.
Like the other alternatives to *National Assembly*, Mounier's
suggestion tried to give an elaborate justification for a speech
act that could succeed only if it needed no justification whatever.
Mounier and Galand's "legitimate," Chapelier's "legally verified," Sieyès's early "recognized and verified" all *asserted* legitimacy when their actual purpose was to *challenge* legitimacy.
What is the purpose of naming the legitimacy of a body whose
claim is that it alone has the right to determine what can be
considered legitimate?

The predecessors of *National Assembly* can also be understood as tortuous efforts to escape from the paradox discussed
earlier: only if the National Assembly were already itself could
it declare what it was, yet it had to make the declaration before
it could be itself. Its authority was simultaneously the precondition and the consequence of its institutionalization, both the
cause and the effect of its existence as a supreme legislative
body. Words such as "legitimate" and "legally verified" sought
to escape the paradox by situating the Assembly's beginning
prior to its declaration that it had begun. The originative moment was the verification of delegates' credentials; the procla-
mation of June 17 only stated what already was. As Derrida

argued about the American Revolution, the early alternatives to *National Assembly* strove to present themselves as not performative but constative, not words that did things but words that named what had already been done.

Even Sieyès's final motion did not completely transcend what can be considered the performative malaise of his colleagues. Recall the language in which he put forward his revolutionary title: "The denomination of *National Assembly* alone befits the assembly in the present state of things." With "things" in their current state, one name and one name alone is appropriate. Choosing a title for the bourgeois delegates is no more arduous than picking a word to name a thing. As a cat is a cat and a dog a dog, so the National Assembly is the National Assembly regardless of who says otherwise. A performative declaration may take its force from a conventional procedure subject to modification, but a constative denomination is accurate solely because of the nature of the world. By defining *National Assembly* as just such a denomination, Sieyès joined his colleagues in refusing to admit that the words they were speaking defined the world they were making.

No one more skillfully exploited the Third Estate's performative malaise than Mirabeau, who defined even the early suggestions for the assembly's name as egregious threats to the established order. To defend his personal choice, *Representatives of the French People*, Mirabeau repeated over and over that this title was not at all alarming. "Recognized and Verified Representatives of the French Nation" was for Mirabeau "a title that frightens" (Buchez and Roux, I, 449). Far better to choose "a name that does not shock, that does not alarm" (I, 466), and "Representatives of the French People" fit the bill nicely. Whereas every mention of legitimacy or the French nation that separated either concept from the king in effect subverted the kingdom, to speak of the French people was only to name a group whose existence was the kingdom's reason for being.

In a memorably perceptive speech defending his position, Mirabeau succinctly formulated what was at stake in the Third Estate's naming practice. "We are all here under the mode of convocation given us by the king. Without doubt, you can and must change it for the future, when you are active; but can you do so today? Can you do so before being constituted? Can you do so in constituting yourselves? By what right can you today exceed the limits of your title? Are you not called as *Estates*?" (Buchez and Roux, I, 447–48). While his colleagues were seeking to hide the discomfiting fact that their power to rename themselves was of necessity its own precondition, Mirabeau made the paradox as pointed as possible. "Before being constituted," the new assembly obviously lacked authority to reconstitute itself as something else. "Called as *Estates*," delegates could not call themselves something else without renouncing their right to gather together and call themselves anything at all. Challenging *what* they were called denied *that* they were called. Mirabeau's play with the Latin root of "convocation" (*con-vocare*) makes the point well. Because "we are all here under the mode of convocation given us by the king," the terms of the royal order are indivisible from the assembly it convened. Altering the terms dissolved the assembly. For Mirabeau, what others were presenting as institution of the new was in fact abolition of the old, and such abolition would make change forever impossible to attain.

Mirabeau's position is analogous to John Searle's contention that a successful declaration guarantees correspondence between its content and the world because of the *prior* organization of the world's conventional procedures. Neither man admits the possibility of a declaration succeeding by overturning all previous declarative rules; yet just that possibility was actualized on June 17, 1789. A speech-act description of the first revolutionary events of the French Revolution requires modifying even the explanation Austin gives for his Rule A.l, that "there must exist an accepted conventional procedure having conventional effect." In Austin's words, "Our formulation of this rule contains the two words 'exist' and 'be accepted' but we may reasonably ask whether there can be any sense to 'exist' except 'to be accepted,' and whether 'be in (general) use' should not be preferred to both. Hence we must not say '(1) exist, (2) be accepted' at any rate" (26–27). According to Austin's view here, a performative's existence depends on its position in a conventional procedure that is already accepted and in general use. But the performative that created the National Assembly also created a procedure that cannot by any stretch of the imagination be considered to have already been in general use. Illocutionary conventions did not precede but followed the illocutionary act. The armed struggle in defense of the National Assembly is striking proof that general acceptance of the Assembly's conventions could not be assumed but had to be imposed.

Austin's play with one of the sentences through which he originated the category of the performative is pertinent. The second example in the first lecture of *How to Do Things with Words* is "I name this ship the *Queen Elizabeth*" (5). The second lecture's consideration of unsuccessful performatives uses the ship to illustrate this commentary:

> Suppose, for example, I see a vessel on the stocks, walk up and smash the bottle hung at the stem, proclaim "I name this ship the *Mr. Stalin*" and for good measure kick away the chocks.... We can all agree
> (1) that the ship was not thereby named;
> (2) that it is an infernal shame. [23]

We can all agree that the ship was not thereby named in the circumstances under which Austin set his anecdote, but we can all equally well imagine different circumstances under which the *Mr. Stalin* would indeed join the world's vessels. As part of a series of revolutionary acts that overthrew the government of Great Britain and established a communist regime in its place, the infelicitous baptism would acquire unimpeachable felicity.

And the imaginary process by which it did so would be identical to the actual rebaptism of June 1789, when *the deputies of the order of the Third Estate* became the *National Assembly*. By all the conventional procedures established in France, the Third Estate could break free of its title no more than the *Queen Elizabeth* could become the *Mr. Stalin*. Yet the break occurred, in the form of a speech act that simultaneously illustrates the analytic value of Austin's categories and displays the need for transcending Austin's assumption of social stability. Only a linguistic philosophy that foregrounds words' power to do things can adequately explain how Sieyès's decree came to be equated with the Revolution itself. But that decree's power also demonstrates that the things words do are subject to collective revision in ways Austin seldom addresses. Whether a ship will be the *Queen Elizabeth* or the *Mr. Stalin* depends on the social reality that follows baptism no less than on the social conventions that precede it.

To claim this is to question one of Austin's fundamental oppositions, that between illocution and perlocution. The former is the act accomplished in the utterance of words, the latter the effect produced after the words have been uttered. Among Austin's clearest examples is the difference between warning and convincing. I can say "The bridge is out" to *warn* you not to take a certain road regardless of whether I *convince* you to turn around. The illocutionary act of warning is independent of the perlocutionary effect of convincing. If your car plunges into the river, my warning's perlocutionary consequences are different from what they would be if you took another road. The warning's illocutionary status, however, remains the same whether you pay attention to it or not. Your fall into the river does not change the fact that warning was indeed given.

Austin equates the illocutionary/perlocutionary distinction with the difference between conventional and nonconventional behavior. "We must notice that the illocutionary act is a conventional act: an act done as conforming to a convention.... Illocutionary acts are conventional acts; perlocutionary acts are *not* conventional" (105, 121). Tone of voice, mode of delivery, propositional content, and many other conventionally defined features identify my "The bridge is out" as a warning. Your drive over the riverbank is, in contrast, not a conventional but a physical phenomenon, qualitatively distinct from illocution. Although you sink and drown, you do not affect the illocutionary definition of the warning I gave.

But so neat a distinction is obviously not applicable to the National Assembly's self-institution, for the illocutionary force

34

of Sieyès's proposition was indivisible from the perlocutionary consequences subsequent to it. Austin returns to his ship to illustrate the difference between perlocution and illocution, and the example remains relevant to 1789. " 'I name this ship the *Queen Elizabeth*' has the effect of naming or christening the ship; then certain subsequent acts such as referring to it as the *Generalissimo Stalin* will be out of order" (117). Yet Louis XVI's convocation of the deputies of the Third Estate had the effect of naming them only to the point at which they declared that their name was itself out of order, that *National Assembly*— in context as outrageous as *Generalissimo Stalin*—was the only appropriate denomination in the present state of things. The illocutionary force of the king's baptism and the bourgeois delegates' counterbaptism was undeterminable until *after* the people of France demonstrated that the latter had prevailed. Perlocutionary events not only followed but also established illocutionary value.

The point Austin slights is this: What happens when conventions are in flux or at war, when only perlocutionary events can reveal the conventions that are operative? As Mirabeau argued, there was no conventional procedure to which the Third Estate could appeal in justification of its right to become the National Assembly. Yet a conventional effect was nevertheless achieved, the National Assembly came to be, and in the process a conventional procedure was *retroactively* inaugurated. The revolutionary actions that followed the National Assembly's birth— the storming of the Bastille, the execution of Foulon and Berthier, the women's march to Versailles—were certainly not conventional in Austin's sense. They were physical, bloody, violent, world-historical. Nevertheless, among their effects was the core of Austin's conventions, the validation of a procedure whose effects are accepted as reality by a mass willing to live the reality it accepts. The major consequence of nonconventional perlocutionary struggle was institution of the conventional protocols synonymous with illocutionary force.

To summarize the discussion to this point: the National Assembly's birth in June of 1789 is both a compelling illustration and an implicit critique of speech-act theory. The bourgeois delegates' change of name had an impact on events that Austin's perspective on words' power to do things best represents. Yet that impact did not derive from the preexisting conventional procedures having conventional effect to which Austin attributes the illocutionary force of performative speech. Conventional procedure and illocutionary force were *simultaneous* creations in June of 1789. Neither counted as reality before perlocutionary—nonconventional—struggle reached a point of resolution. Austin's insistence that social conventions alone grant words the capacity to alter the world is essential to the strength of his theory. But he tends to assume that the conventions responsible for speech's active power are static and set, and the French Revolution is one among many periods of social upheaval that show conventions to be as malleable as any other human creation. Like the choice between "National Assembly" and "Third Estate," those between *Queen Elizabeth* and *Mr. Stalin* or "the present king of England" and "the present king of France" are unproblematic only if we assume that the social conditions under which the choice is made are not subject to change. Because social conditions not subject to change have yet to be encountered in human history, the clean separation between illocutionary force and perlocutionary effects cannot survive. Austin's belief that conventional speech acts and nonconventional, nonspeech acts are distinct runs counter to his fundamental insight that saying and doing are indivisible.

That insight is central to the other Austinian thesis that will figure prominently in this book, the ultimate identity of constative and performative speech. In the drama of *How to Do Things with Words*, quite the most dramatic element is Austin's gradual dissolution of the performative/constative distinction with which he began. Austin's early lectures define the constative as a statement about reality, the performative as a transformation of it. The later lectures relentlessly shred that opposition to bits. To the question, "What then finally is left of the distinction of the performative and constative utterance?" (145), Austin's implicit answer is "Nothing worth thinking about." The conventional procedures that absolutely delimit what we can do with words also have determinant impact on what we can say with words.

A prototypical performative rite, the marriage ceremony, can help summarize why Austin first posited the category of the performative and how he came to the conclusion that the category was not worth preserving. As I argued in the Introduction, Austin is unique among linguistic philosophers because of his constant recognition that truth is much more than a simple matter of accurate reference. For some of Austin's colleagues, the statement "John and Mary are married" is of philosophical interest because of the conditions that would apply in an effort to determine its accuracy. Such statements are to be evaluated by comparing their propositional content to a situation unaffected by the proposition's enunciation. John and Mary might or might not be married, but their relationship would remain the same irrespective of any words I might say about it.

To philosophical inquiries about this constative language, Austin contrasted his own concern with performative propositions whose enunciation has direct and immediate impact on their referents. If we compare "John and Mary are married" to "I now pronounce you husband and wife" as spoken to John and Mary during their wedding, major differences are immediately apparent. First, it is senseless to ask the classic truth-value questions about "I now pronounce you husband and wife." This sentence is not true or false depending on its descriptive validity but it is effective or ineffective—felicitous or infelicitous—depending on its extralinguistic environment. Second, if the sentence is felicitous, it has an effect on John and Mary far beyond anything attributable to a constative description of them. No one who has ever been through a difficult divorce needs instruction on the power of the marital performative to exemplify words that do things in profound, durable, and overweening ways. Third, Austin's Rule A.1, the necessity for conventional procedures having conventional effects if speech is to perform felicitously, deserves its prominent position. Apart from the conventions that institutionalize marriage in our society, "I now pronounce you husband and wife" does nothing except disturb the air with sound waves. The acts in speech acts proceed solely from the collective agreements through which humans regulate their interactions with one another.

So far, the performative/constative distinction is straightforward. Austin has no trouble providing many other examples of words that affect reality by virtue of their position in a society's conventional delineation of its members. The problem arises when we realize that the conventional procedures invoked in Rule A.1 are no less critical when words describe reality than when they transform it. The socially specific marital conventions giving force to "I now pronounce you husband and wife" surely also determine the truth of "John and Mary are married." Because the latter statement's accuracy depends on the former's efficacity, a single conventional procedure grounds both. Whether my purpose is to perform a marriage or announce one, I am equally dependent on the social consensus that decides what marriage is.

If that consensus breaks down, the truth value of a constative disappears at the same time as the illocutionary force of a performative. For an orthodox Catholic, John and Mary are not married if they were previously divorced despite secular inscription of the wedding. In many countercultural settings, John and Mary are married despite the absence of such a secular inscription. No less than a performative pronouncement of marriage, a constative description of one relies absolutely on the precise, socialized agreements Austin codified in Rule A.1.

Imagine a courtroom in which a sensational, televised trial is taking place. At a certain moment, the appropriate official walks into the front of the room and says "Court is now in session." Immediately afterward, a television reporter in a glass booth at the rear of the room says exactly the same words. The first utterance is a clear instance of the performative, the second no less clear an instance of the constative. The court official opens judicial proceedings, the reporter states that proceedings have been opened.

Highly elaborate conventional procedures empower the official's words to begin the court's work. Although the reporter's words have no function in that work, which would proceed in the same way if the reporter said nothing, the constative "Court is now in session" relies for its *truth* on the collective processes responsible for the *force* of the same sentence's performative utterance. Why do the court official's words do something real? Because a social totality recognizes their authority to act. Why do the reporter's words say something true? Because verbal authority recognized by a social totality suffices to transform the world. If the official's words do not act, the reporter's words do not represent. Whether used to do things or to say things, language derives its value from collective acquiescence before those things that it says and does.

Consider what happens when acquiescence is not collective. Over the last few years, trials of dissident activists in this country and abroad have often produced scenes in which an inaugural "Court is now in session" elicited not respectful silence but an uproar punctuated by shouts of "This is not a court!" or "We do not recognize these proceedings!" In such a situation, what does the hypothetical reporter say? Is court in session or is it not? Because the answer depends on which set of conventional procedures the reporter recognizes as valid, his or her constative utterance is inescapably implicated in acute social conflict. Far more than a mere assertion of objective fact, description of court activity is completely dependent on the conventional rules legitimating (or de-legitimating) execution of court activity.

Courts and marriages illustrate the interdependence of verbal truth and verbal performance with special clarity because both invoke the same social protocols whether they are mentioned in a description or in a pronouncement. If it is objected that such examples cannot be generalized, the response is a challenge to come up with a pure constative, one that does not appeal to the same conventional procedures identifying the performative. Russell's difficulties in arguing that denotation depends merely on the referent's existence are typical, for denotative accuracy is always also a matter of collective agreement. Assume that instead of saying "John and Mary are married," one seeks to escape the performative by using the simple declaratives "John is a man" or "Mary is a woman." The questions of what a man is and what a woman is, however, are currently the stakes of social struggle far more intense than the conflict over what constitutes a marriage. To make any statement including the words "man" and "woman" is willy-nilly to accept or reject certain ideological conventions that make each occurrence of those words a performance. Assessing the truth of "John is a *man*" inevitably entails assuming a stance toward the conventions and contentions that determine felicity at the same time as fact. Balzac's representation of the conventions of sexual vocabulary at work is the subject of the next chapter.

In Austin's ultimate conception, the constative/performative opposition breaks down precisely because fact and felicity are indistinguishable. *How to Do Things with Words* began by investigating a class of speech in which the true/false opposition had to be replaced by that between felicity and infelicity and ended by discovering that truth and falsity were themselves the effect of performative felicity conditions. "Is the constative, then, always true or false? When a constative is confronted with the facts, we in fact appraise it in ways involving the employment of a vast array of terms which overlap with those that we use in the appraisal of performatives. In real life, as opposed to the simple situations envisaged in logical theory, one cannot always answer in a simple manner whether it is true or false" (142–43). As opposed to logical theory, real life takes place in society, and societies survive by imposing their conventions on their members. Because truth is one of those conventions, the constative must be appraised exactly as we appraise the performative, by evaluating the circumstances surrounding it as well as the proposition it conveys.

As a result, truth is a politically defined concept with the same charge and the same prickliness as freedom.

It is essential to realize that "true" and "false," like "free" and "unfree," do not stand for anything simple at all; but only for a general dimension of being a right or proper thing to say as opposed to a wrong thing, in these circumstances, to this audience, for these purposes and with these intentions. . . . The truth or falsity of a statement depends not merely on the meanings of words but on what act you were performing in what circumstances. [145]

Instead of the performative's opposite, the constative is one of its subcategories. What I call truth, like what I call freedom, inserts me in a network of political forces and collective actions that align me with or against the other members of a social formation. To state what is true requires performing as well as observing, and the standards for truth's performance derive from the conventional procedures of Rule A.1.

Speech-act theory's conflation of the constative and performative suggests an explanation of the tortuous mental and lexical posturing that accompanied the Third Estate's transformation into the National Assembly. As discussed earlier, bourgeois delegates were achingly reluctant to accept the fact that changing their name required wresting declarative authority from the king and undermining the basic institutions of the Old Regime. Their diffidence was obvious in their attempts to pretend that the performative revolution actually being accomplished was nothing more dangerous than constative recognition of objective reality. Mounier's *Legitimate Assembly of the Representatives of the Larger Portion of the Nation, Acting in the Absence of the Smaller Portion* tried to overcome performative malaise by denying that a performative was even being employed. The truth was that the representatives of the larger portion of the nation were acting in the absence of representatives of the smaller portion, and no one would maintain that simply stating the truth threatens social order. An analogous feeling seems to underlie the curious wording of the Tennis Court resolution of June 20, 1789, by which the performative "Be it resolved" clauses did little more than paraphrase the constative "Whereas" clauses. Such a rhetorical structure attenuates subversion by phrasing it so as to repeat a neutral description. Since it was a fact that the National Assembly was called to make a constitution, what harm could come of declaring that the National Assembly was called to make a constitution?

The language Sieyès chose to name the National Assembly is an exemplary instance of constative/performative interpenetration: "The denomination of *National Assembly* alone befits the assembly in the present state of things." Since it is the prerogative of the constative to describe the present state of things, choice of a name dictated by that state became less a historic seizure of power than an unbiased assessment of the world. Throughout the creation and defense of the National Assembly, the political consequences obvious in performative speech concealed themselves behind the apparent neutrality of constative denomination of things as they were.

The strategy could work, however, only if constative speech and performative speech were effectively in opposition, and the core of speech-act theory is that no such opposition exists. Rather than blunting the political impact of their declarative gestures, the members of the National Assembly were actually demonstrating that use of constative speech is in and of itself a political act. The same forces arrayed against Sieyès's motion to impose *National Assembly* contested his vision of "the present state of things." The same reactionary groups that sought to invalidate the Tennis Court resolution derided the resolution's preamble. Mounier could have increased the length of his proposed title by any number of placidly descriptive terms, but the title would have remained a mortal threat to established order. As Austin said, a statement's truth depends "on what act you were performing in what circumstances" (145). In the circumstances that developed into the French Revolution, the act performed by a statement of truth was fully politicized. Assertion of objective fact and usurpation of political power were separate moments in a single social struggle.

Like the force of the National Assembly's declarations, therefore, the truth of its statements was determinable only after perlocutionary events took their historic course. The reservations expressed earlier about the assumption of stable conventions in Austin's discussion of performative felicity also apply to evaluation of constative modality. If truth depends on what act you were performing in what circumstances, then a change of circumstances is also a change of truth. In the reactionary view, the Tennis Court preamble was false for the same reason that the Tennis Court resolution was invalid: both confounded principles essential to the social and political system equated with the eternal order of the world. Conversely, the extralin-

42

guistic events that established the resolution's authority at the same time grounded the preamble's factuality. Had the French Revolution been quashed in the summer of 1789, bourgeois representation of the world would have been false for the same reason that bourgeois transformation of the world would have been impossible. Because the French Revolution was not quashed, the criteria for constative accuracy shifted with the criteria for performative efficacity. What a group can say with words varies with the fortunes of its social battles just as much as what it can do with words.

Those battles must consequently attain some degree of at least provisional resolution before a statement can be assessed for accuracy. To return to the courtroom disrupted by activist rebellion, consider the situation created when court is taken over by armed soldiers. If those soldiers are loyal to the regime in power, a constative "Court is now in session" is true. If the soldiers are revolutionaries, however, that same sentence is untrue. Revolutionary events determine the fidelity of verbal representation as well as the success of verbal performance.

Austin's Rule A.1 once again: there must exist an accepted conventional procedure having conventional effect. The kicker is the word "accepted." Although Austin uses it to imply that a conventional procedure's authority must precede its invocation, revolutions make it obvious that authority can also be a retroactive production. The speech-act vision of language has at its core an awareness that all the acts of speech derive force from the protocols by which a collectivity regulates itself. Periods of social turmoil reveal that those protocols are variable and cannot be isolated from the events that follow their successful or aborted application. In the early summer of 1789, the accepted effect of a royal declaration was what Searle called "guaranteed correspondence" between the king's words and reality. That the guarantee was worthless could be seen only after the correspondence failed to materialize. A coherent social concept of language requires awareness that conventional procedures are determined by dynamic processes that never reach a point of stasis.

Bakhtin and his collaborators installed that recognition at the base of their vision of language. According to Bakhtinian principles, equating language's force with an *accepted* conventional procedure denies the truth that all linguistic phenomena simultaneously include acceptance *and rejection* of the procedures allowing language to signify. Even so small a linguistic unit as the single word spoken by a single speaker carries within itself the ideological thrust of vast collective conflict. V. N. Voloshinov: "Each word, as we know, is a little arena for the clash and criss-crossing of differently oriented social accents. A word in the mouth of a particular individual person is a product of the living interaction of social forces" (41). Sieyès's *National Assembly* did nothing more than make apparent the clash and crisscrossing of social conflicts that was latent but nonetheless determinant in more deferential terminology such as *deputies of the order of the Third Estate*. Conflict is overt in some utterances, concealed in others, but none can communicate without full involvement in the endless dialogics of social coexistence.

Dialogics is contradiction, and revolutions bring contradiction to the surface. Stable societies with a serenely hegemonic ideology mask contradiction by enshrining certain words as incontrovertible. Voloshinov's vision of the difference between language's appearance in a stable and a tumultuous social situation applies directly to the Salle des Menus Plaisirs before and after the Third Estate's transfiguration.

> The ruling class strives to impart a supraclass, eternal character to the ideological sign, to extinguish or drive inward the struggle between social value judgements which occurs in it, to make the sign uniaccentual.
>
> In actual fact, each living ideological sign has two faces, like Janus. Any current curse word can become a word of praise, any current truth must inevitably sound to many other people as the greatest lie. This *inner dialectic quality* of the sign comes out fully in the open only in times of social crises or revolutionary changes. In the ordinary conditions of life, the contradiction embedded in every ideological sign cannot emerge fully because the ideological sign in an established, dominant ideology is always somewhat reactionary and tries, as it were, to stabilize the preceding factor

44

in the dialectical flux of the social generative process, so accentuating yesterday's truth as to make it appear today's. [23–24]

For partisans of the Old Regime, *deputies of the order of the Third Estate* was a string of inert signs devoid of "inner dialectic quality." The name suited to its referent, it was a truth not datable as yesterday's or today's. Violent rejection of that string of signs uncovered both the contradiction embedded in it and the temporal character of truth in society. The French Revolution began by performing what Voloshinov identified as the prime semiotic function of "social crises or revolutionary changes," revealing that all signs contain a social message indivisible from their meaning, that no sign can signify neutrally.

Voloshinov and Austin share visceral knowledge of the dominance of collective processes in determining how words can do things. What Voloshinov adds to Austin is a clear, pointed sense that those collective processes are the creation of social conflicts never finally resolved, at best temporarily suspended. Austin's attitude toward accepted conventional procedures precludes Voloshinov's emphasis on the "dialectical thrust of the social generative process" that evacuates as well as empowers the conventional procedures of a given community.

Austin and Voloshinov are at one, however, in insisting that communal conventions authorize constative as well as performative utterances. Voloshinov's statement that "any current truth must inevitably sound to many other people as the greatest lie" amplifies Austin's insight that "real life" makes it impossible to determine in a simple manner whether a statement is true or false. Voloshinov's opposition between yesterday's truth and today's is implicit in Austin's conviction that truth depends on "what act you were performing in what circumstances." For both men, speech acts in society, not in the artificial environment of logical theory or linguistic rationalism. For both men, the effects words produce depend absolutely on the collective dynamics enclosing their utterance.

Voloshinov's emphasis on the capacity of revolutions to bring words' participation in collective struggle into the open thus confirms the appropriateness of an Austinian reading of the

National Assembly's institution. In June of 1789, the conflict over language displayed with special clarity the interdependence of language and conflict in human coexistence. The argument in this book is that the revolutionary events that followed June of 1789 repeated the display in an extraordinary range of ways and with an almost limitless variety of examples. In his history of the French language, Ferdinand Brunot devotes twelve hundred pages to the lexical transformations produced by the Revolution and Empire. Enveloped in the events that created modern Europe, words became different from what they were before. Almost all the words and word families that Brunot examines could serve to illustrate the points made in this discussion of *National Assembly*. The French Revolution was, among many other things, an immense proving ground for the contention that speech acts according to how its users interact. Words became weapons, offensive and defensive, and the weapons' effectiveness was in direct correlation to the political fortunes of the groups which (and for which) they named.

Since Brunot himself admits that his twelve hundred pages are inadequate to the full linguistic panoply of the French Revolution, it would be futile even to try to show here how many revolutionary moves and countermoves reiterated the lessons of *National Assembly* through different lexical material. Let me nevertheless try to indicate the scope of sociolinguistic upheaval during the Revolution by recalling what happened to the manifestations in French of three linguistic universals, designations of time, those of space, and the first- and second-person forms necessary for every dialogic interaction.

A comparison can help show the extreme social awareness underlying the Revolution's attitude toward inherited words for space and time. I am writing this on a January Monday in 1986 in New York, New York. In the ordinary conditions of life, that information is just that, information. It conveys no ideological message, bespeaks no communal hierarchy, performs no ceremony of adherence to a political position. Yet the French Revolution saw in the equivalents of the date and place I just named a host of pretexts for militant revolutionary action. Monday is the day of the moon, January the month of Janus, and the two genitives both recall and affirm religious practices inimical to the liberation of free citizens. Analogously, to mention the year 1986 is to agree that the central event in human history is the birth of Christ and thus to accept the teachings and power of the Church that explains why the event is central.

Naming the place where I am writing is no less politically retrograde than naming the time. "New York, New York," by twice uttering the name of a British nobleman and his property, represents as unquestioned the aristocratic ideology according to which people and property are legally identical. In Voloshinov's terms, the neutral information about my writing was in actuality a thoroughgoing strategy for stabilizing a preceding factor in the social generative process.

It was in order to counter that strategy that the French Revolution renamed days, weeks, months, years, and places. The central event in human history became not the birth of Christ but the creation of the French Republic One and Indivisible, and every moment in the Republic's life acquired a new name purged of all echoes of outmoded social systems. As with the calendar, so with the map. Kings, queens, saints, and churches became geographic nonentities and were replaced by the new language of a new political compact. Paris sections illustrate what happened throughout the nation. Place Louis XIV became William Tell, Place Royale became Indivisibilité, Notre Dame was supplanted by Raison, Henri IV by Révolutionnaire, and Bonnet Rouge appeared where Croix Rouge had been. The toponyms that seem inert in normal times acquired intense ideological charges when the French Revolution renamed the divisions of French territory.

Impositition of new names for the units of space and time was often an important ceremonial occasion. Debates about the revolutionary calendar include some of the most memorable speeches before the Convention, for example, and the renaming of a section or a village provided a forum for the Revolution's concept of popular democracy. Less solemn but perhaps more momentous were the many changes that affected the verbal intercourse essential to everyday life, of which the most ubiquitous was proscription of the singular *vous* in favor of the more fraternal *tu*. Considered an obsequious second-person equivalent to the royal we, singular *vous* was quickly perceived as a powerful lexical tool for making hierarchical social positions indispensable components of every vocal exchange. The movement against it—*tutoyeurs* was one of the synonyms for "revolutionaries" during the turbulent years that followed 1789—was a critical aspect of the Revolution's ideological battles. To say anything to another person required choosing words and pronouns perceived as working for or against the collective drive toward starting history over again.

So abbreviated a discussion of the ways in which the conflict over *National Assembly* continued in other forms can make its point because the point is neither how many lexical changes occurred nor which semantic fields they affected. What matters is simply that choice of words was during the French Revolution a statement of political principle; verbal representation was equated with reform or reaction. From this perspective, it is immaterial that the associations with "Janus" and "New York" mentioned earlier are archaic and dead and that sans-culotte militance against analogous terms seems distant from serious political activity. This distance itself illustrates how hard it is to assimilate Austin's insight into the feats that language performs. Regardless of whether "Croix Rouge" and "vous" were authentically conservative, "Bonnet Rouge" and "tu" authentically progressive, a mass recognized those words and uncounted others as full participants in its struggle for sociopolitical identity. During the Revolution, the French language became an essential component of the conventional procedures established, defended and contested by all the groups constituting the French nation.

This book's thesis is that the realist novel developed an especially powerful means for representing the inextricable connections between verbal expression and group dynamics that figured among the French Revolution's object lessons for the world. The works by Balzac, Stendhal, and Zola examined here simultaneously perform and analyze the kind of speech acts manifest in *National Assembly* and the lexical ferment that succeeded it. The realist insight can be summarized in this way: a major task of language in human existence is to embody particular ideologies so as to make them appear universal. Stated in such terms, this insight reads like a hackneyed reformulation of the fundamental discovery that contemporary continental critics have applied to almost every literary genre over the last two decades. This resemblance is by no means accidental, and the following pages will accept and affirm the discoveries of critics who have shown that the textuality of realist prose is intimately connected to that of genres often defined as antithetical to the realist project. This connection does not dismantle but accentuates realist specificity, which I take to be not an impossible fidelity to a sociohistorical referent but a successful activation of the process by which sociohistorical collectivities make language appear referential. This book considers realist fiction to be a literary form that corresponds to Austin's ultimate concept of the constative, and it sees the French Revolution and its aftermath as the historical precondition for that form's invention.

Each of the following chapters takes a major realist text as simultaneously exposing an absence and articulating a presence. The absence, denounced time and again in structuralist and poststructuralist inquiry, is that of the founding, grounding reality that stands as the incontestable justification of the sign's existence while evincing no need for the sign in order to impose its own existence. The presence, more often suggested than contemplated in the contemporary human sciences, is that of the reality performed and produced when signs successfully collaborate with the conventional procedures that organize a collectivity. The epistemological preconditions for Austin's speech acts are identical to those for the unlimited semiosis and free play of the signifier foregrounded by continental linguistic theory. The identity fails in epistemological postconditions, for Austin concentrates on the things words do in a fashion that is as determined as deconstruction's concentration on the things immaterial to their doing. The realist difference defended here is an analogous insistence that language is at one and the same time independent of objective reality and inextricable from social reality.

49

The French Revolution played out the dialectic of presence and absence throughout the tumultuous period inaugurated by the National Assembly's institution of itself. Like the royal word in June of 1789, a long series of political languages was in subsequent years shown to be absolutely incapable of expressing reality without collective ratification of their descriptive authority. Yet every such loss of nominative power was accompanied by the introduction of other names acquiring referential validity as spectacularly as the original articulation of *National Assembly*. Realist texts make the same dual demonstration: no form of language is inherently valid, every form of language can become absolutely valid when a group integrates its conventions among the forms of communal interaction. To paraphrase Victor Hugo on his fellow poets, the novelists of the nineteenth century are the children of the French Revolution.

Such an assertion raises the question of why the offspring's gestation period was so lengthy. If the concept of language and reality inscribed in French realism is that enacted during the French nation's rapid dismissals and investitures of distinct social systems, why was the realist novel the product not of revolutionary upheaval but of the comparatively stable period that followed it? Why did fifteen years of "restoration" precede Balzac and Stendhal's invention of a literary form adequate to the interpenetration of speech and acts during collective annihilation of what was being restored?

The answer lies in the dual character of the realist constative as an expression no less true than arbitrary, no less motivating than unmotivated. The furious pace of revolutionary change was a compelling demonstration that no eternal reality guaranteed the eternal truth of representations of the real, but that pace also raised the problem of whether reality retained any of the attributes traditionally assigned it. The Restoration elided the problem when it prevailed and endured. By installing itself as if there had been no interruption of the monarchy's thousand-year continuity and by making the installation succeed (at least on the second try), the Restoration performed a reality that seemed to have recovered its constitutive stability. Although they were crushingly refuted by the facts of history, the Restoration's claims for itself nonetheless effected an irrefutable fact of history. The characters with whom Balzac and Stendhal populated the Restoration are the same admixture of unjustified and incontrovertible substance. As constative beings, they embody both revolutionary dismemberment of referential thought and reactionary imperatives to think referentially. Constative denomination is a verbal performance that conceals its performative nature, and the realist constative manifests the Restoration's successful concealment as much as the Revolution's spectacular performances.

2

Castration, Speech Acts, and the Realist Difference: S/Z versus SARRASINE

Of the many reasons why *S/Z* is the most cited of Roland Barthes's works, the one of primary significance here is its relentless demonstration of the need to rethink realism as a genre. *S/Z* is a magistral argument against traditional assumptions that the specificity of realist prose lies in its faithful representation of a precise referent. In terms of the dialectic between presence and absence characteristic of the realist constative, Barthes concentrates exclusively on the absence. The purpose of this chapter is to examine how Balzac's text uses that absence to inaugurate a presence, how *Sarrasine* converts linguistic performance into constative reality by aggressively denying language's connection to objective truth and affirming its expression of social truth. The literature of the constative begins where the literature of the referent disappears.

Wholly persuasive in its dismantlement of referentiality, Barthes's view of *Sarrasine* ignores constative reference. Whereas Barthes understands Balzac's castrato in the abstract, as a figure for undecidable sexual identity, *Sarrasine* represents the castrato in society, as a figure for collective creation of identity. Before defending that assertion in detail, let me summarize Barthes's argument and the critical positions it implies.

According to the received ideology of realist representation, the semantic opposition between "man" and "woman" is in a mimetic relationship to the physiological contrasts between male and female human beings. Barthes reads *Sarrasine*'s elimination of the referential basis for the man/woman distinction as a first step toward destroying the assumptions necessary for readers to believe that realism designates anything at all. Asexuality brings all other distinctions to grief; such granite oppositions as those between life and death, inside and outside, heat and cold follow the male/female binary into oblivion. In Barthes's metaphor, castration is contagious; sexual uncertainty decertifies the basic principle of realist denotation, the belief that the denoting word is distinct from other words, the denoted referent unlike other referents. By displaying one realist text's relentless iconoclasm before the oppositions essential to representationality, Barthes seems to expunge realism from among the operative terms in the critical lexicon.

The most interesting challenge to Barthes's reading of *Sarrasine*, Barbara Johnson's *The Critical Difference*, does not restore the distinctions necessary to realist denotation. Instead, Johnson argues that Barthes is not sensitive enough to the force with which Balzac makes distinction unutterable. For Johnson, the "critical difference" is that the word "castration," which dominates *S/Z*, never appears in *Sarrasine*. Barthes "fills in the textual gaps with a name" (11) and thus assigns unequivocal meaning to a text that actually offers nothing but a blank where meaning should be. In Johnson's view, Balzac not only makes denotation impossible, he refuses even to attempt it; by making the attempt for him, Barthes distorts the Balzacian accomplishment. "On the basis of this confrontation between a literary and a critical text, we could perhaps conclude that while both involve a study of difference, the literary text conveys a difference from itself which it 'knows' but cannot say, while the critical text, in attempting to say the difference, reduces it to identity" (Johnson, 12). The identity principle conventionally associated with realist representation construes words as the world and equates a literary text with extraliterary reality. By emphasizing that Balzac's tale about a castrato uses its words to expose the *absence* of extraliterary reality, Barthes detaches realism from its primary epistemological claim. Johnson further dissipates the supposed individuality of realist fiction by focusing on *Sarrasine*'s refusal to refer even to the absence of anything to which to refer. Balzac's representational prose, no less than Mallarmé's antirepresentational poetry, is in eccentric orbit around a void.

That void is essential to the argument that speech-act theory furnishes a way to defend realism's classic definition as the literature of social specificity. As exemplified in *S/Z*, the critical debate on realism posits a dichotomy between radical indeterminacy and complete certainty. Textual meaning is either guaranteed by an extratextual referent to be fixed, stable, and unquestionable or detached from every extratextual presence to become shifting, ephemeral, and unknowable. From the point of view of such critics as Lukács, realism represents a world ontologically independent of the terms in which it is represented; for Barthes and Johnson, ontological independence is a myth concealing the fact that representation can never depict anything except its own artifices. Realism is either true or dynamic, and it is just this dichotomy between truth and dynamism that speech-act theory invalidates. From an Austinian perspective, constative meaning stabilizes through the creative work of collective conventions, not through the passive conjunction of a name and a thing. The reference that matters is not the *source* but the *product* of verbal performance, and Balzac's castrato is the ideal illustration.

From a referential perspective, the antonymy between the words *man* and *woman* is unproblematic because men and women are unmistakably different from one another. Barthes demonstrates that the castrato's function in *Sarrasine* is to invalidate the referential perspective by detaching the text from every possibility of unmistakable difference. What Barthes does not emphasize, however, is that *Sarrasine* maintains the verbal opposition between "man" and "woman" against its own refutation of the opposition's extraverbal validity. Balzac represents his unsexed creature first as a fully sexed male, then as a fully sexed female. In eighteenth-century Rome, la Zambinella looks, acts, sings, and makes love just like a woman. In nineteenth-century Paris, the same character is a man. Although the referential basis for these sexual identities is missing, constative representation of the identities themselves is unimpeachable. *Sarrasine* simultaneously deconstructs received ideas about denotation and employs classically denotative discourse with confident authority. Sexually marked language is no less straightforward for the accompanying demonstration that sexual marking is purely arbitrary. Like *National Assembly*, the name for a man or a woman takes validity solely from the conventions with which it interacts.

Barbara Johnson faults Barthes for saying what *Sarrasine* leaves unsaid. If we turn from textual gaps to sexual names, however, the objection becomes Barthes's attempt to unsay what *Sarrasine* says. Whenever Balzac designates the castrato through standard constative forms for expressing sexual identity—the words *man* and *woman*, gender-specific adjectives, pronouns, and articles—Barthes announces a "lie," a "false trail," or a "feint" and puts things back in (dis)order. The castrato's first sexual identification in *Sarrasine*, for instance, is a perfectly unequivocal three-word sentence, "C'était un homme," it was a man. Barthes immediately comments: "The oldster, in fact, is not a man; there is thus a feint from discourse to reader" (48; all translations from Barthes and Balzac are my own). When the castrato is la Zambinella and the text calls her a woman, Barthes's response is the same: "There is a false trail, for Zambinella is not a woman" (140). It would be easy to multiply examples. To almost all specifications of the castrato's sexual identity, Barthes reacts by categorically negating what the text affirms: "The oldster, in fact, is not a man.... Zambinella is not a woman."

The objection to these interpolations is obviously not that they are wrong; since a single character is both a man and a woman, each unequivocal label makes the other dizzyingly equivocal. The problem is rather that Barthes's commentary assimilates realist discourse to the postmodernist formula that Samuel Beckett named in *The Unnamable*, "affirmations and negations invalidated as uttered" (291). *Sarrasine* certainly negates all its affirmations of sexual identity, but not "as uttered," not before establishing a context in which their constative validity is secure. In Rome, la Zambinella is the quintessence of womanhood, and the text names her accordingly. In Paris, she becomes a man, and the text represents him exclusively through masculine language. "It was a man" could stand as a minimal example of the classic representational sentence, as the zero degree of what used to be called the transparent discourse of realist fiction. By dissociating *man* and *woman* from the physiological difference that the words are thought to name, *Sarrasine* makes it impossible to assume that realist prose actually allows readers to see through it to the world beyond. Nevertheless, the text's representationality endures, and it is no more legitimate to contend that its sentences undo themselves than to take them as the unmediated reproduction of objective reality.

What prevents *Sarrasine* from unraveling the classic form of Balzacian discourse as it demolishes classic understandings of the Balzacian universe? The text's choice to validate social reality at the same time that it denies objective reality, to defend the constative while expelling the referential. The castrato's different designations are held apart because they are applied in different countries at different times. By continually negating textual affirmations of gender, *S/Z* defines the castrato as *between* male and female, as neither one *nor* the other: "a kind of average of the sexes, equidistant from masculine and feminine" (215). By rigorously maintaining sexual identity as socially articulated, *Sarrasine* defines the same character as *successively* female and male, as both one *and* the other. In the abstract, a castrato embodies indeterminable meaninglessness; in Balzac's prose, a castrato acquires determinate meanings from alternative sets of social conventions. A man and a woman come into being within a text which also denies that their being has any basis beyond the forms of its representation.

Recall Barthes's correction of "It was a man," Balzac's original statement of the castrato's gender: "The oldster, in fact, is not a man." That *in fact* is highly questionable, for the narrative structure of *Sarrasine* is a fully developed demonstration that words do not name in *fact* but only in communities. In Balzac's *Illusions perdues*, Vautrin summarizes his lessons to Lucien de Rubempré thus: "So the fact is no longer anything in itself, it is wholly in the idea others form of it" (700). *Sarrasine* illustrates Vautrin's point. It is immaterial that the castrato is not in fact a man; the fact in itself is nothing. As constative terms, *man* and *woman* label not facts but conventions, not physical realities but social fabrications.

The distinction is obvious in one of the alternate descriptions of the character first presented with "C'était un homme." "C'était la femme avec ses peurs soudaines, ses caprices sans raison, ses troubles instinctifs, ses audaces sans cause, ses bravades et sa délicieuse finesse de sentiment" (It was woman with her sudden fears, her whims without reason, her natural anxieties, her daring without cause, her bravado, and her delightful delicacy of feeling; lexia 439). The traits here predicated on *woman* specify that the word names a received idea rather than an anatomical condition, designates not "the fact in itself" but "the idea others form of it." "It was a man" and "It was woman" are both true because neither asserts anything except the arbitrary classificatory operations by which a sociolinguistic community identifies and names its members.

S/Z defines "It was a man" as a sentence in a void. "Here it is impossible to attribute an origin, a point of view to the utterance. This impossibility is one of the measures that allow us to appreciate a text's plurality. The more the utterance's origin is irretrievable, the more the text is plural" (48). "It was woman" is comparable: "The sentence's origin is indiscernible" (178), which is of course why Barthes chose the sentence to ground his classic article on the death of the author. For Barthes, this kind of concealment of language's origins is a major achievement of the postmodernist exploration of language's possibilities called *écriture:* "The being of *écriture* (the meaning of the work that constitutes it) is forever to prevent an answer to this question: *Who's talking?*" (146). *S/Z* consequently sets *it was a man/ it was woman* among the textual elements through which *Sarrasine* aligns itself with the language games that identify the writerly literature of our modernity.

This argument is emblematic of the steps through which *S/Z* eliminates the generic specificity of realist prose along with the philosophical assumptions formerly invoked to define it. *Sar-*

rasine unquestionably detaches its masculine and feminine vocabulary from a genital referent. But Barthes contends that *man*,
woman, and their variants are consequently detached from every
conceivable ground to vanish in an imploding collapse of sense,
and yet *Sarrasine*'s sexual vocabulary simply does not collapse.
Whereas Barthes defines the origin of "It was a man" as irretrievable and that of "It was woman" as indiscernible, Balzac
identifies the origin of those and all other socially communicative terms as the social group that makes them communicative.
In what amounts to a demonstration of this point, *Sarrasine*'s
first designation of la Zambinella's sex occurs in Italian. "The
appearance on stage of the *prima donna*" (lexia 216) is also the
appearance in words of her gender. When, in the two sentences
immediately following that double entrance, *Sarrasine* denotes
la Zambinella as "she" and as "this woman," it inaugurates a
naming operation that is not a lie but a cross-cultural translation. In the constative sense of "is" that I take as the core of
Balzac's realism, the character who is a man in nineteenth-
century Paris is also a woman in eighteenth-century Rome.

First made female through the theatrical practice of the papal
states, la Zambinella remains female through the collective stratagem of a theatrical troupe. The social invention of the manhood
attributed to the mysterious figure in the Lanty household is less
blatant but more durable. In both the milieus where it is applied,
sexual vocabulary represents a convention instead of a reality.
The crucial point, however, is that the textual force of convention survives textual elimination of reality. Barthes encapsulates
his reading of Balzac in these terms: "*Sarrasine* represents the
very turmoil of representation, the unregulated (pandemic) circulation of signs, sexes, fortunes" (*S/Z*, 222). The most striking
fact about *Sarrasine*, however, is that what ought to be the agony
of representation is rather the smooth, readerly discourse of a
classic realist text. What could become the unregulated circulation of signs refuses to do so; it provides instead a compelling
demonstration of Austin's thesis that societies regulate constative meaning without concern for referential truth.

The death of *Sarrasine*'s title character is the supreme display
of meaning's localization within its social matrix: a Frenchman

applies the interpretive conventions he grew up with to a milieu where they are invalid, takes the signifiers of feminine gender as the proof of female sex, and is murdered for his mistake. Barthes, however, sees Sarrasine's failure to recognize that meaning has frontiers as the global annihilation of meaning itself: "By copying Woman, by taking her place above the sexual bar, the castrato will transgress morphology, grammar, discourse, and Sarrasine will die of this abolition of meaning" (*S/Z* 72). That quotation exemplifies the vision of language as an absolute which *S/Z* substitutes for *Sarrasine*'s vision of language as a social instrument. Morphology, grammar, and discourse stand above the community that uses them to produce autonomous meaning. As one of the paradigmatic oppositions essential to meaning, the sexual bar separates two Platonic ideals, one of which is here named Woman with a capital W. By straddling so basic a semantic division, the castrato makes meaning impossible and leaves realism indistinguishable from postmodernism.

But in *Sarrasine*, the sexual barrier and the morphology, discourse, and meaning it supports remain intact within the frontiers assigned them. The castrato replaces neither the Platonic ideal of Woman in eighteenth-century Rome nor the Platonic ideal of Man in nineteenth-century Paris. *Sarrasine* depicts both societies as giving their members precise sexual definitions which depend only on Austin's Rule A.1, the existence of a conventional procedure having conventional effect. Although the referential basis for Balzac's representation of the sexual barrier is nonexistent, the representation itself is integral and coherent. Objectively, the castrato is unsexed; textually and socially, s/he is what s/he is named.

Derivation of naming procedures from social settings continues even beyond the point where Sarrasine learns from Prince Chigi that the woman he loves is not a woman.

Prince Chigi could surely have spoken for a long time, Sarrasine was not listening to him. An atrocious truth had penetrated his soul. He was struck as if by a thunderbolt. He stood motionless, eyes fixed on the supposed singer. His fiery gaze had a kind of magnetic attraction for Zambinella, for the *musico* finally looked toward Sarrasine, and then the heavenly voice broke. He trembled! An involuntary murmur from the crowd, which his lips held to him, compounded his discomfiture; he sat down and broke off his song. [lexias 472–78]

All of Zambinella's feminine designations proceed from the foreign phrase that originally brought her femaleness into the text, the *prima donna*. All of her masculine designations proceed from the foreign phrase through which the narrative voice effects a gender change, the *musico*. In each case, an alien expression institutes a new convention rather than a claim of truth. At the beginning of the preceding passage, masculine pronouns designate a male character, Sarrasine: *he was struck*, *he stood motionless*. At the passage's end, the same pronouns designate a character who is not male, Zambinella: *he trembled*, *he sat down*. The "thunderbolt" blasting Sarrasine does not disturb *Sarrasine*, which continues to employ gender-specific language with calm assurance. Like *man* and *woman*, *he* and *she* are constative, not referential, and dissolution of referents is not pertinent to constative expression.

For Barthes, however, dissolution of referents annihilates all expression, and Zambinella's loss of womanhood leaves language an empty noise. Here is *S/Z*'s commentary on Sarrasine's discovery of castration: "There is produced in the subject what might be called a *paradigmatic collapse*: two terms separated by the strongest of distinctions...are suddenly brought together in the same person...meaning, statutorily grounded in difference, is abolished; there is no more meaning, and this subversion is fatal" (191). Sarrasine does indeed experience paradigmatic collapse when he learns that Zambinella is also the opposite of Zambinella. But Barthes takes this individual catastrophe as all-encompassing, and the text's persistent defense of social semantics appears as a persistent denial of all semantics: "there is no more meaning." A single character's disorientation becomes a textual attempt to forbid orientation absolutely. Instead of the victim of his own ethnocentrism, Sarrasine is in *S/Z* a figure for the impossibility of ever centering oneself in any way. For Barthes, meaning is "statutorily grounded in meaning." For Balzac, the statutes of meaning admit no categorical imperatives but vary with the group in which meaning circulates. Difference is an illocutionary performance not a prelocutionary principle.

Whereas Balzac repudiates language's referential value while affirming its constative force, Barthes reacts to the repudiation without attending to the affirmation. *Man* and *woman*, *he* and *she* appear in *Sarrasine* not as signs attached to a referent but as conventional constituents of a conventional procedure. Shut off from the applicable conventions by ignorance of Italian customs and language—an ignorance the text repeatedly foregrounds—Sarrasine assumes that he can name as he always has. Although the result is undeniably fatal, what dies is not language but certain assumptions about it. If objective principles disappear, constative meaning replaces them; if the referent is absent, the signified is textual bedrock. *Sarrasine* and Sarrasine, a text and one of its characters, have diametrically opposite visions of how sense is made, and the character's death affirms the life of the linguistic vision he failed to assimilate.

Substitution of constative conventions for referential truth is the inaugural gesture of *Sarrasine*, which opens on a series of conversations in which Parisian society displays its perfect indifference to abstract semantic scandals so long as concrete collective protocols are observed. The castrato appears in a milieu already characterized by speech with no referential pretensions whatever. Besides displaying dubious masculinity, for instance, the decrepit intruder in Parisian gatherings seems to be something other than a human being. Like the man/woman opposition, that between human and inhuman loses its objective ground as *Sarrasine* assigns the castrato a series of traits designated in Barthes's semantic code as *ultra-temps*, *sur-nature*, or *extra-monde*. Yet this supernatural creature inhabits a society which in Balzac's representation made semantics a branch of economics and defined its members through the single semantic feature of wealth. As a result, even the Prince of Darkness would become human if he were rich enough. " 'So what if he's the devil,' said a few adaptable youths. 'They give marvelous parties' " (lexia 19). Like the male/female binary, the difference between natural and supernatural is not an objective fact but a collective fabrication. Referential language pretends that the oppositions it denotes exist in the world. Constative language asserts only the tautology that denotative opposition constitutes denotative opposition. Because what is inhuman in itself becomes human in any group that interprets and names it as such, *Sarrasine*'s "it was a man" identifies species just as reliably as gender.

The contrast between Balzac and Barthes is perhaps most obvious in their respective attitudes to the opposition between life and death. For Barthes, Sarrasine's doubts about whether a castrato can be alive imply that no classification can be dependable: "The loss of desire takes the castrato below all life and all death, *outside of every classification*; how do you kill what is not classed? How do you reach what transgresses not the inner order of the sexual paradigm . . . but the very existence of difference, generator of life and of meaning; the full horror is not death but that classification of life and death is broken off" (202). The castrato, "outside the sexes" (53) as well as "below all life and all death," is thus the ultimate denotational scandal. Each step in Barthes's argument is on its own terms consistent, coherent, and compelling. But its terms all preclude attending to the social ground that *Sarrasine* attaches to such binary concepts as life and death, human and inhuman, man and woman. The Paris where the most unnatural of creatures continually appears in the most natural of settings is also the Paris where death is not a physical but a socioeconomic event. In the words of the same anonymous Parisians who humanize Satan, "to kill a man's fortune is sometimes worse than killing the man himself" (lexia 49). When Sarrasine's encounter with a castrato teaches him that the barrier between life and death is shifting and deceptive, his lesson merely reiterates what Balzac's readers already know perfectly well.

Like other Parisians, Balzac's narrator responds to the perception of life and death coexisting not with a writerly explosion of unlimited semiosis but with a readerly meditation on social custom.

> ah! c'était bien la mort et la vie, ma pensée, une arabesque imaginaire, une chimère hideuse à moitié, divinement femelle par le corsage.
>   Il y a pourtant de ces mariages-là qui s'accomplissent assez souvent dans le monde, me dis-je.

> Oh, it was indeed life and death, my thought, an imaginary arabesque, a chimera hideous to the midpoint, divinely female in its torso.
>   "Yet there are marriages like that taking place rather often in society," I said to myself. [lexia 91]

The occasion for this astounding passage is the narrator's vision of the decrepit old castrato and the vibrant young marquise in physical contact. The hallucinatory spectacle they create stands as a figure for all the text's games with difference destroyed. Life and death, male and female, heat and cold, beauty and ugliness combine in what Barthes interprets as the end of meaning and the end of the rhetorical figure embodying the distinctions on which meaning depends, Antithesis. "Antithesis is the wall without an opening. To pass through this wall is transgression itself. Subjected to the antithesis of inside and outside, heat and cold, life and death, the old man and the young woman are rightfully separated by the most inflexible of barriers, that of meaning. Consequently all that brings these two mutually repelling sides together is wholly scandalous (the starkest of scandals: that of form)" (71). What is for the narrator the *social* banality of arranged marriages is for Barthes the *formal* scandal of opposites intertwined. An "imaginary arabesque" in thought, the vision of life and death together is also an everyday occurrence in society. The narrator's epistemological crisis consequently dissolves in ideological reassurance, and meaning retreats from the abyss to return to the world of its users. " 'Yet there are marriages like that taking place rather often in society,' I said to myself." Balzacian prose converts the transhistorical infamy of oppositional disarray into the narrator's insight that semantic array is one historical variable among others.

The conversion is stylistic as well as substantive, syntactic as well as semantic. On perceiving the other as the same, the narrator's thought first seems to be in apposition with life and death, then detaches itself to spin metaphors too fast for verbs: "c'était bien la mort et la vie, ma pensée, une arabesque imaginaire, une chimère hideuse à moitié, divinement femelle par le corsage." On recalling that the same and the other combine rather often, the narrator promptly recaptures control of grammatical subordination. Within the reversible discourse of postmodernism, the two parts of this sequence might have reciprocal impact; fantastic thoughts and expressions could consequently elude repression by their more seemly successors. But the realist constative gives the sequence a different effect. Prescribed *dans le monde*, repression works.

The prototypically Balzacian use of *le monde* is a one-word synopsis of the affinities between Austinian thought and realist representation. The truth of constative expression is restricted to a specific community but appears to that community's members to be universally valid. This same combination of restriction and universality is apparent in the dual meanings of *le monde*, both "the world" and "polite society." The word that continually recurs in *La Comédie humaine* to name the setting in which identity is performed has as its alternate definition everything that has no need for performance because it simply exists. A single term designates the locus of a precise set of conventions and evokes the nonconventional reality of brute physical facts. Balzac's *monde* and Austin's Rule A.1 communicate the same insight into the product of social protocols made indistinguishable from the world as it was before all social organization.

The protocol that rescues the narrator from his imaginary arabesque is the rite of marriage, the classic example of performative speech that Austin chooses for his first illustration of the category and Searle uses to exemplify "institutional" facts. Before the words "I now pronounce you husband and wife," no husband and wife are present. After those words, a married couple has come to be by coming to be spoken. The tight con-

nections between the marriage ceremony and a speech-act theory
of meaning also appear pertinent to the marquise's remark when
she subsequently observes a deconstructive arabesque blending
the centenarian castrato with a woman as beautiful and young
as she herself, Marianina. " 'What does that mean?' my young
companion asked me. 'Is he her husband?' " (lexia 138). At two
separate points in the text, a figure of undetermined meaninglessness, the castrato, seems to absorb and obliterate the exquisitely determined figure of meaning at its most dependable,
a beautiful young woman. Each time the dissolution of meaning
in itself provokes a reference to meaning in society, to the ritual
of marriage in which words do not refer but perform. Deconstruction of language's objective value immediately becomes
affirmation of its illocutionary force.

Whereas marriage is the *locus classicus* for speech-act theory's
assertion that social sense is always consubstantial with social
conventions, Barthes takes marriage as a metaphor for the absolute impossibility of sense. In the symbolic code of *S/Z*, the
"marriage of the castrato" (57, 59, and so on) effected by textual
blending of contraries produces intolerable semantic chaos:
"The depths are expelled, as in vomiting. That's what happens
when we subvert the arcana of meaning, when we abolish the
sacred separation of paradigmatic poles, when we erase the bar
of opposition, ground of all 'pertinence.' The marriage of the
young woman and the castrato is twice catastrophic" (72). For
Barthes, the foundation of all semantic pertinence is the paradigmatic barrier. For Balzac, the paradigmatic barrier's disappearance is not pertinent to the semantics of a group that has
chosen to ignore it. Where the critic perceives a catastrophic
evacuation of meaning, the narrator perceives a phenomenon
recurring rather often. *Sarrasine* simultaneously subverts the
deep structures of meaning and defends meaning's surface manifestations in classically representational fashion.

Marriage demonstrates with special clarity the dialectic between the words that do things and the conventions that define what they do. The formulas for effecting a marriage are
not eternal but historically variable, and this specificity is
central to the marriage allusions elicited by the blending of

life and death in *Sarrasine*. *S/Z* reads the same blending ahistorically and posits the breakdown of an eternal and universal essence, Antithesis with a capital *A*. "Antithesis separates for all eternity...Antithesis is the figure of opposition as *given*, eternal, eternally recurrent: the figure of the inexpiable. Every alliance of two antithetical terms, every mixture, every conciliation, in a word every passage through the wall of Antithesis thus constitutes a transgression" (33–34). Yet the narrator's move from the imaginary arabesque of obliterated antithesis to the social commonplace of arranged marriages functions precisely to deny that any transgression has occurred. In Balzac's prose, the constitution of sense is not given, eternal, and eternally recurrent but produced, historical, and historically unique. Symbolically assigned two wives (Marianina and the marquise) in Restoration Paris, the castrato also has two husbands (Prince Chigi and Cardinal Cicognara) in eighteenth-century Italy. In both settings, formal scandal is irrelevant to social custom. The same collective voice that pronounces individuals men and women also has the authority to pronounce them husband and wife.

Sarrasine's socially determined marriage of contraries manifests the irrelevance of abstract semantic structure to concrete semantic practice by denying representation's orthodox definition while perpetuating its orthodox form. This combination of denial and preservation is the core of Austin's ultimate definition of the constative. The central opposition is between meaning and truth, two contraries that Barthes considers indistinguishable in realist prose. In the section of *S/Z* called "signified and truth" Barthes writes: "Every process of meaning is a process of truth; in the classical text (depending on a historical ideology) meaning is confused with truth, signification is the road to truth; if there is a way to succeed in *denoting* the old man, his truth (as castrato) is immediately unveiled" (68). This assimilation of meaning and truth comes apart when we recall that Balzac's text does succeed, repeatedly and masterfully, in denoting the castrato without revealing the truth of castration. The process of sense in *Sarrasine* is not the road to reality but the expression of what society accepts as real.

The realist distinction between sense and truth, representation and reality, is explicit in *Sarrasine*'s meditation on the function of money in Restoration Paris.

Là, les écus même tachés de sang ou de boue ne trahissent rien et représentent tout. Pourvu que la haute société sache le chiffre de votre fortune, vous êtes classé parmi les sommes qui vous sont égales, et personne ne vous demande à voir vos parchemins, parce que tout le monde sait combien peu ils coûtent. Dans une ville où les problèmes sociaux se résolvent par des équations algébriques, les aventuriers ont en leur faveur d'excellentes chances.

There even coins stained with gore or mud reveal nothing and represent everything. Provided high society knows the extent of your fortune, you are classed among the sums that are equal to you, and no one asks to see your pedigree, because everyone knows how little it costs. In a city where social problems are solved by algebraic equations, adventurers have excellent prospects in their favor. [lexia 26]

Prefiguring Saussure, Balzac affirms the correlation between the social function of money and the social function of signs. Like *francs* and *écus*, *man* and *woman* "reveal nothing and represent everything." Whether monetary or verbal signs effect it, representation is insistently defined as arbitrary and unmotivated and is delineated no less insistently as solid and unquestionable. Classed among the sums equal to him, the castrato receives names that make no epistemological claim beyond their conformity to the conventions accepted by the group in which they circulate. Semiotic and social problems alike are resolved "by algebraic equations," the defining feature of which is that the equation holds regardless of the referent attached to the algebraic "x" or "y." Money's abject referential failure is immaterial in its compelling constative success.

As with words, Barthes's commentary on Balzacian money brilliantly glosses the failure while ignoring the success. "Once (says the text) money 'revealed,' it was an index, it reliably designated a fact, a cause, a nature; today it 'represents' (everything); it is an equivalent, a currency, a representation, a sign

... The difference opposing feudal society to bourgeois society, index to sign, is this: the index has an origin, the sign has none ... Succeeding the feudal index, the bourgeois sign is metonymic turmoil" (46–47). Unlike the meaning of a sign, that of an index derives from the objective reality of its referent. A feudal index reliably designated a fact because the fact was causally connected to the index's existence as a unit of meaning. By contrast, the meaning borne by signs comes not from the things they denote but only from the meaning system in which they figure. Because causal connections extend not outward to the world but inward to other signs, what is in reality has no connection to what is meant in signification.

Sarrasine meticulously protects the meaning of society's signs from the effects of society's renunciation of indexes. Where Barthes sees "metonymic turmoil" in money's central position for bourgeois life, Balzac depicts money as the instant resolution of social problems, not an impediment to but a facilitation of socially requisite classificatory operations: "You are classed among the sums that are equal to you." Whereas *Sarrasine* and *S/Z* agree that the index has an origin the sign lacks, they disagree dramatically on the consequences attached to the origin's disappearance. In the critical analysis, those consequences are all-consuming. In the realist narrative, they are nonexistent.

Barthes's definition of money as a "metonymic turmoil" constitutes a thematic kernel finally expanded to produce his concluding definition of *Sarrasine* as a whole. "This catastrophic collapse always takes the same form: that of unchecked metonymy ... *Sarrasine* represents the very turmoil of representation, the unregulated (pandemic) circulation of signs, sexes, fortunes" (221–22). Comparable parallels regularly recur in *S/Z*, which often identifies the void of money with the void of castration: "Without origin and without destination, (Parisian) Gold is a substitute for the emptiness of castration" (55); "this money is empty, like the state of castration" (47). Although Barthes uses it to evacuate money, this illuminating identification can equally well express constative plenitude. As the defining feature of a commodity is the priority of exchange value over use value, so the defining feature of the castrato is the priority of social denomination over objective reality. Although it expresses nothing, money represents everything. Although they reveal nothing, the castrato's sexual names represent all that needs to be known about him. The catastrophic collapse of objective truth is ineffectual beside the social ratification of constative naming.

Within a certain Marxist discourse, the thematic implications that *Sarrasine* assigns both money and castration might figure in an effort to reverse Barthes and validate the triumph of realism at the base of a referential reading of Balzac by Friedrich Engels. Instead of understanding Parisian money as a "substitute for the emptiness of castration," such a reading might argue that castration is merely a surrogate for money. My purpose is not to reverse Barthes's hierarchy, however, but rather to argue that *Sarrasine* makes all such hierarchal orderings unacceptable. Money is not the base on which the metaphorics of castration stand as superstructure, nor is castration a symbolic nucleus spinning off monetary variants on its own indeterminacy. Both exemplify the same constative view of *collective* meaning. *Man* and *woman*, *écus* and *francs* coalesce in the fundamental realist discovery that the social resonance of any sign is invariably a performative act in which the absence of a solid referent is irrelevant to the presence of a solid signified.

The solidity of the signified produced in verbal performance is the most important lesson in Austin's conflation of constative and performative speech. If a materialist approach would tend to ignore that solidity because it lacks a firm determination in the last instance, the deconstructionist perspective of *S/Z* posits an unchecked metonymy prohibiting determination in any instance whatever. The rich deconstructionist discussions of speech-act theory that followed *How to Do Things with Words* have in general viewed Austin's collapse of the constative/performative distinction as Barthes views Balzac's collapse of the referential claims of realist prose. The strategies imposed by foregrounding the undecidable have tended to suggest that Austin's shift from opposition to assimilation is reversible, that difference somehow survives demonstration of sameness. In the following excerpt from his discussion of Rousseau's *Social Contract*, for instance, Paul de Man considers the contrast between performative and constative language to be as significant as their identification.

> The tension between figural and grammatical language is dupli-
> cated in the differentiation between the state as a defined entity
> (Etat) and the state as a principle of action (Souverain) or, in
> linguistic terms, between the constative and the performative func-
> tion of language. A text is defined by the necessity of considering
> a statement, at the same time, as performative and constative,
> and the logical tension between figure and grammar is repeated
> in the impossibility of distinguishing between two linguistic func-
> tions which are not necessarily compatible. [270]

So brief an excerpt from a single essay cannot possibly do justice to the subtlety of de Man's appropriation of Austin. Like figure and grammar, performative language and consta-tive language are for de Man both "not necessarily compati-ble" and impossible to separate. Nevertheless, the language that here represents the incompatibility of Austin's major categories remains disquieting because it suggests that "the necessity of considering a statement, at the same time, as performative and constative" produces the tension of logical undecidability. In *Sarrasine*, however, that necessity is in the end the perfectly logical consequence of a statement's exist-ence as a statement. Whereas de Man here strategically fore-grounds the opposition between performative and constative in the early sections of *How to Do Things with Words*, that opposition becomes irrelevant when Austin makes verbal statement a subcategory of verbal performance, when what words say becomes one of the many things they do.

De Man's allusions to speech-act theory presuppose Jacques Derrida's critique of Austin in "Signature Event Context." In Derrida's view, Austin's attempt to exclude "non-serious" (Aus-tin, 122) citation of performative utterances from consideration established an indefensible hierarchy of values that comes close to invalidating the entire Austinian understanding of speech, of acts, and of their combination. The Derridean critique of Austin will be discussed in more detail in the following chapter. Let me simply note here that Derrida's strictures do not apply to Austin's breakdown of the constative/performative opposition, which Derrida in fact marshals in support of his argument that the opposition between serious and nonserious speech acts is indefensible as well.

> From this point of view one might examine the fact recognized by Austin that "the *same* sentence is used on different occasions of utterance in *both* ways, performative and constative. The thing seems hopeless from the start, if we are to leave utterances *as they stand* and seek for a criterion."...It is the graphematic root of citationality (iterability) that provokes this confusion, and makes it "not possible," as Austin says, "to lay down even a list of all possible criteria." [325]

The vital Derridean category of iterability is wholly compatible with Austin's insistence that constative truth is as conventional a production as performative authority. The points of contention between Derrida and Austin do not involve the latter's conviction that a spoken fact is only one among many sorts of speaking performances.

But to recognize the performative nature of statements of fact in no way prohibits the facts performed from being true. Some recent critics have so celebrated Austin's contempt for the "true/false fetish" (151) that language's ability to express social reality disappears along with its ability to express objective reality. Shoshana Felman's analysis of Molière's *Dom Juan* in *The Literary Speech Act*, for example, identifies the constative function as a theological concept utterly dependent on the objective solidity of divine truth.

> What is really at stake in the play—the real conflict—is, in fact, the opposition between two views of language, one that is cognitive, or constative, and another that is performative. According to the cognitive view...the sole function reserved for language is the *constative* function: what is at stake in an utterance is its correspondence—or lack of correspondence—to its real referent, that is, its truth or falsity. [26–27]

Felman here identifies the constative with the referential, the truth that language performs with the truth independent of language. Yet it is just this identification that Austin finally makes untenable. Throughout Felman's *Literary Speech Act*, "constative," "cognitive," and "referential" are taken as interchangeable terms. In Austin, however, language's absolute separation from objective reality goes hand in hand with its absolute dependence on social reality. The cognitive and referential disappear, but the constative remains. Abolition of the cognitive entails acceptance of the distinction between successful and unsuccessful performance characteristic of the constative. The absence of the referent is irrelevant to the words that signify its presence.

Barthes's antipathy to the realist vision of a constative meaning that retains its force while renouncing its referent is apparent in his influential category of the reality effect, the "effet de réel." This is from Barthes's essay on the discourse of history: "Like any discourse with 'realistic' pretensions, that of history believes it controls a semantic schema with only two terms, referent and signifier.... In other terms, in 'objective' history, the 'real' is never more than an unformulated signified, sheltered behind the apparent omnipotence of the referent. This situation defines what we could call the *reality effect*" ("Le Discours de l'histoire," 74). Realism, a discourse claiming to be purely referential, can leave its signified unformulated because it pretends that signification has no need for structure.

Barthes's article entitled "L'Effet de réel" repeats and expands the earlier definition of the basic realist device, "the *direct* collusion between a referent and a signifier: the signified is expelled from the sign" (88). Barthes's two examples are the barometer on Mme Aubain's piano in Flaubert's *Un Coeur simple* and the small door at the rear of Charlotte Corday's cell in Michelet's history of the French Revolution. Such objects are remarkable because their textual inscription is textually nonfunctional. Unassimilable within any semiotic schema, they stand within the text but neither contribute to its signifying strategies nor combine with its combinatorial elements. Structures of meaning leave them out, they are "the irreducible residue of functional analysis" (87).

To resolve the quandary posed by the apparent meaninglessness of such concrete details, Barthes modifies the concept of realism's unformulated signified. Because there can be no direct association between an object's textual designation and its physical existence, *barometer* and *small door* cannot *denote* the things they name. Nevertheless, those notations can and do *connote* the existence of things to which names are attached. In so doing, they effect things' world within texts' words: "Suppressed from realist enunciation as denotational signified, the 'real' comes back in as connotational signified" (88). Instead of designating the constituents of reality, the prosaic accumulation of accidental details suggests the reality they constitute. The irreducibly residual elements which functional analysis leaves out all have a single, compelling function: to connote the truth of the elements that functional analysis explains. "Flaubert's barometer, Michelet's small door finally say nothing but this: *We are the real;* it is the category of the 'real' (and not its contingent contents) that is then signified" (88). Michelet's door appears to open onto the world because it does not open onto anything in his text. Detached from the rest of his story, Flaubert's barometer seems to register the pressure of the atmosphere surrounding us. Realism effects reality not by naming it but by indefatigably amassing words that name nothing else.

Numerous critical adaptations testify to the analytic value of Barthes's reality effect. Nevertheless, the insistence on a binary opposition between textual realism and textual signification precludes concern with what I take as central to the realist enterprise, fictional representation of constative signification in the absence of referential specificity. The two-term semantic schema—signifier and referent—that Barthes associates with realism leaves no place for the constative signified. "Let us call *realism* any discourse that accepts utterances accredited by the referent alone" (88). That definition from "L'Effet de réel" is at the origin of the analysis of *Sarrasine* in *S/Z*. As an entity accredited by the referent alone, the castrato is in fact undefinable and hence unrealistic. As an entity accredited by the signs denoting him, however, the same character is perfectly definable and hence perfectly realistic. Without any pretense of referential accuracy, *Sarrasine* makes and defends the classic realist claim of social truth.

Realism can therefore be understood not as practicing but as exposing the reality effect, the process through which a collectivity pretends that its signs are the unmediated representation of referents. Revealing nothing but representing everything, cut off from reality but inextricable from perception of it, the language of *Sarrasine* both denounces ideological mystification and represents its smashing success within an ideological community.

One of Barthes's most consistent stylistic techniques is to enclose words that might be taken to designate reality in quotation marks. Among the definitions of realism in "L'Effet de réel," for instance, is this: "the pure and simple 'representation' of the 'real,' the naked relation of 'what is' " (87). In Barthes's next two paragraphs, the word *réel* occurs eight times, invariably in quotation marks. This technique serves to define the real as a spoken rather than an objective category, but a speech-act approach understands the name assigned the category as no less significant for its typographical identification as speech. Realism, the literature of the "real," of reality as spoken, takes as its fundamental concern how the "real" becomes the real, how reality as spoken determines reality as experienced. *Sarrasine*, the text that introduces a castrato by saying *It was a man* is also the text that shows why it should have said *It was a "man."* Its choice to eliminate the quotes does not constitute Barthes's expulsion of the signified but rather manifests collective *infusion* of a signified in the absence of a referent. The "real" deserves its name because social consensus suffices to make its quotation marks disappear.

In *S/Z* as in the articles preceding it, what is "real" in realism are those textual elements deprived of meaning: "To make it 'real,' you have to be precise and insignificant at the same time" (75). Applied to *Sarrasine*, this conviction produces an amalgam of inert reality effects and pulsating *écriture*, each of which has clear affinities with the use of "constative" and "performative" by such critics as Felman. In Austin's original formulation, language's constative function does appear to entail the direct collusion of a signifier and a referent, and the assimilation of language's performative capacities to exercises in sheer textuality is a common trope in contemporary criticism. If, however, we view the performative and constative functions through Austin's ultimate vision of the social conventions that are prerequisite to what words say as well as to what they do, the disparate styles of *Sarrasine* assume radically different implications. Constative reality effects are to performative textuality what constative gender is to a castrated referent, the demonstration that language performs in society, that speech acts according to collective protocols. One instance of what *S/Z* identifies as a reality effect can illustrate the point.

As we saw earlier, a striking instance of the castrato's symbolic marriage comes when he touches his beautiful relative Marianina. Signifiers exult in their liberation from meaning, and the wall of Antithesis consubstantial with meaning crumbles into dust. Just before the symbols of life and death separate, the castrato gives Marianina a beautiful ring, which the young girl laughingly puts on her finger without bothering to take off her glove. Barthes characterizes this move from explosive textuality to pedestrian narration as reintroduction of the reality effect in a work which just moved past reality. "The laughter, the glove are reality effects, notations whose very in-significance authenticates, signs, signifies the 'real' " (88).

Classification of Marianina's glove and laughter as reality effects illustrates the consequences imposed by Barthes's stance toward realist discourse. Resolution of social problems through transfer of a commodity becomes a meaningless gesture detached from every social ground. Consider the series of events in their readerly sequence. A ring of great cost is exchanged. The beneficiary of the exchange expresses her delight by laughing while—as if to display the irrelevance of use value to the ring's status as a commodity—she puts it not on her finger but on her glove. Narrative and thematic development from the ring to the laugh seems obvious, yet Barthes posits an uncrossable barrier between them, the barrier separating full textuality from empty notation. At the same time, this empty notation stands as the essence of realism, the accumulation of signifiers freed from the organizational constraints imposed on a signified. When Barthes's *Sarrasine* is, as it is here, a constative text, it has repudiated the social origins of constative meaning. When its symbolic or semantic codes comment on the nature of meaning, they dissolve the constative altogether.

Earlier, the castrato joined the marquise in an imaginary arabesque that dissolved the wall of Antithesis, and the narrator's speech intervened to define the dissolution as no more transgressive than a socially convenient marriage. Here the castrato joins Marianina in another figure of antithetical collapse, and the narrative proceeds to recount a commodity exchange with comparably benign effects. *Sarrasine* "authenticates, signs, signifies the 'real' " as just that, the real that is what people say it is. The authentification of this "real" comes not in opposition to but in collusion with the coded operations through which a community's members effect and ratify its ontology.

The crucial category of the reality effect, operative at several other important points in Barthes's analysis of *Sarrasine*, always makes a similar point. It allows *S/Z* to accept the generic specificity of realist discourse without compromising its vision of *all* literary expression as the transcendent flight of *écriture*. Through this strategy, the realist project textualized in *Sarrasine* becomes a mixture of literature as properly understood and something that is not only not literature but is not even signification, periodically interpolated utterances accredited by the referent alone. On the one hand, Balzac's prose belongs among the great denunciations of the banalities imposed by slavish representation of the "real"; on the other, that prose incorporated the system of immobile formulas through which the "real" always imposes itself on the world.

Barthes's reality effects are thus the diametrical opposite of Austin's constative, the conventional effect of a conventional procedure. Like the structures of signification, the structures of convention obviously cannot include entities defined as the irreducible residue that remains after every form of structural understanding has been exhausted. The preceding discussion of

Marianina's glove and laughter illustrates what seems to me an incontestable gain produced by rejecting the reality effect in favor of the constative when considering realist prose: understood as social rather than objective, reality no longer has to be left out of textual analysis. Signifying the "real" becomes the same sort of process as signifying anything else, Antithesis and its annihilation, Woman and her ideological conceptualization, money and its disruptive metonymies. Without in any way homogenizing the text, attention to its constative vectors finds a continually reinforced coherence where *S/Z* posits a continually interrupted textuality. Rather than stopping *écriture* dead, the reality effects in *Sarrasine* are so many reminders that the operations of *écriture* entail parameters no less exigent than those governing realist representation itself.

A final extract from the catalog of reality effects provided by *S/Z* can illustrate the consistent importance of conventionality in *Sarrasine*'s references to the "real." Lexias 545–47 state that the painting of a beautiful young man hanging in the Lanty home is Vien's version of the figure that Sarrasine sculpted while inspired by his love for la Zambinella. Reacting to the textual specification that Vien executed his portrait in 1791, Barthes provides this description of the referential code at work: "REF. Chronology. In fact, the information is dulled, it cannot be linked to any other guidepost … it is a pure reality effect; nothing's more 'real,' people think, than a date" (213). What makes the date 1791 a *pure* reality effect? Its absolute dissociation from every other textual component. Reality effects necessarily fail to signify because they cannot be correlated with any other elements of the signifying system they infiltrate.

But surely this reasoning neglects a major correlating function of Vien's portrait, its status as a link (with its subject, the only link) between the two halves of *Sarrasine*, the narrating world of nineteenth-century Paris and the narrated world of eighteenth-century Rome. Furthermore, this painting of a man—but one who is too beautiful to be a man (lexia 114)—based on a statue of a woman—but one who is not really a woman—is a pictorial correlative of the multiple commentaries on verbal representation of gender that constitute the dominant movement in *Sarrasine*. The concrete connection between the society that is recounted and the society that recounts it is also a dynamic synopsis of the varied naming procedures that distinguish each society from the other.

The portrait's central thematic and narrative situation suggests the possibility that its date might signify as well. What the date invokes is the French Revolution and the great divide in human history discussed in the preceding chapter. Vien copied Sarrasine's statue in 1791, the midpoint between 1789 and 1793, between the Third Estate's inaugural uprising and the sans-culottes' cataclysmic dictatorship. In 1791, a revolution became the Revolution, and the word for it began to convey previously unsuspected semantic and material possibilities. In 1791, the fleeing royal family's capture at Varennes made constitutional monarchy a hopeless fantasy, aristocratic intransigence made destruction of all feudal privilege inevitable, and papal, imperial, and royal declarations set France against the rest of Europe. In 1791, what Barthes called "the difference opposing feudal society to bourgeois society, index to sign" (47) became a world-historical conflict in which the nature of the sign was simultaneously a stake and a weapon. Vien painted his portrait of a "woman" as a "man" in the year when France as a nation was coming to appreciate the value of putting those words and all others in the quotation marks that traditionally attach a word's meaning to its users.

If this kind of discussion of events that occurred in the year named by a textual date sounds like an argument for referential rather than constative understanding, the response is simple. Regardless of what actually happened in the French Revolution, the significant point in Balzac's prose is how a collectivity *represents* what happened. Crucial to representation as practiced in the narrator's world of Restoration aristocracy is the idea that the Revolution destroyed the conventions essential to civilization and stability. Throughout *Sarrasine*, the words that name are totally dependent on the protocols of a group of namers, and the word for any revolutionary year calls all this group's protocols into question. Balzac's depiction of conventions solidifying the words that society uses to identify its members includes at a crucial juncture a historical reminder of why the solidity established is no more than conventional. The French Revolution, a vast collective affirmation of the vision of reality as social production animating *Sarrasine*, both joins and divides the worlds in which *it was a man* and *it was woman* acquire and lose their truth.

"Chronology" rather than "history" is Barthes's term for the coded function exercised by such signs as 1791: "REF. Chronology. In fact, the information is dulled, it cannot be linked to any other guidepost." This concept of disconnected chronological information stands in relation to history as the reality effect stands in relation to constative representation. In each case, the critical distinction is between what humanity endures and what it performs, between facts in themselves and facts in society. From a speech-act perspective, historical allusions in realist fiction mark the conventional procedures being applied to produce the conventional effects being written. The connotations of a historical term such as "1791" are a powerful reminder of the necessity of understanding *all* terms as bearing a signified specific to the ideology of their users. Realist history invokes less the acts preceding language than the acts within it, acts that take effect as constituents of a precise social environment most succinctly designated through chronological coordinates that are themselves ideologically active.

In "Le Discours de l'histoire," Barthes defines exactly the vision of history that I am arguing for here, but he denies that realist discourse can incorporate it.

Nietzsche already said it: "There are no facts in themselves. We always have to start by introducing meaning before there can be a fact." ... So we come to this paradox that regulates all pertinence in historical discourse (by comparison to other kinds of discourse): the fact always has a purely linguistic existence (as term of a discourse) and yet everything occurs as if this existence were purely and simply the "copy" of another existence, situated in an extra-structural field, the "real." [73]

Nietzsche's conviction that there are no facts in themselves but only facts in language is not the refutation but the precondition of realist history as a constative enterprise. Because it is part of discourse, the fact is conventional in its essence, which means that its field and its reality can never be extrastructural. Although history does indeed have only a linguistic existence in realist prose, the demands that its existence be recognized are imperious and multiple. To situate those demands in discourse does nothing to lower their volume. Like *man* and *woman*, "1791" and all the other historical markers in *Sarrasine* derive their force not from a referent but from a convention. That being said, however, the next step is to appreciate the power with which the convention works.

In *The Political Unconscious*, Fredric Jameson takes *S/Z* as the quintessence of a critical discourse that Marxism must both incorporate and leave behind.

> The aim of a properly structural interpretation or exegesis thus becomes the explosion of the seemingly unified text into a host of clashing and contradictory elements. Unlike canonical post-structuralism, however, whose emblematic gesture is that by which Barthes, in *S/Z*, shatters a Balzac novella into a random operation of multiple codes, the Althusserian/Marxist conception of culture requires this multiplicity to be reunified. . . . The current post-structural celebration of discontinuity and hererogeneity is therefore only an initial moment in Althusserian exegesis, which then requires the fragments, the incommensurable levels, the heterogeneous impulses, of the text to be once again related. [56]

Despite the considerable difference between Jameson's history and Austin's conventions, I think it is legitimate to assert that speech-act theory also furnishes a way simultaneously to cancel and preserve the poststructuralist dismantling of realist prose. *Sarrasine* is indeed what *S/Z* shows it to be, an adamant denial of the referent and a relentless assault on orderly signification. But it is also something else, a readerly narrative of how meaning functions in history despite its wholly spurious grounds for doing so.

If the subject of realism were facts in themselves, then the sexual vocabulary of *Sarrasine* would necessarily produce what Barthes claims it does, "a general collapse of economies," of above all "the economy of language, ordinarily protected by the separation of opposites" (*S/Z*, 221). If no such collapse occurs, it is because the separation of opposites is a purely ideological operation, and in Balzac's realism ideology is a localized project. Barbara Johnson criticized Barthes for "fill[ing] in the textual gaps with a name" and saying what Balzac left unsaid. By also unsaying what Balzac said, Barthes fills in *Sarrasine*'s historical and social gaps as well, and the realist difference disappears along with the reality it was once thought to name. That difference resides in textual representation of clashing and contradictory elements, of heterogeneity and discontinuity, as they are brought into homogeneous ideological harmony by the force of constative signification. The language that performs in *Sarrasine* and in the three realist texts discussed in the following chapters is the language that manifests collective control of a recalcitrant world.

3

The Father Loses a Name:
Constative Identity in LE PÈRE GORIOT

In one of its many applications of the standard techniques for novelistic realism developed in the eighteenth century, the text of Balzac's *Le Père Goriot* attributes its origin to the discoveries made by one of its characters. According to this device, the information about Goriot's past life given the reader comes from Eugène de Rastignac's research into his fellow pensioner's background. "Without the observations to which his curiosity led him and the skill with which he gained entry to the drawing rooms of Paris, this tale would not display the colors of truth it no doubt owes to his astute mind" (17; all translations from Balzac are my own); "Rastignac wanted to learn about the earlier life of père Goriot and assembled reliable information" (101). Functioning like a footnote to a legitimately historical narrative, such accreditations are a classic means for speciously asserting the referential status of a nonreferential work.

Rastignac's first information about Goriot's biography comes during his celebrated visit to the vicomtesse de Beauséant, when he listens to a long speech by Mme de Langeais. Here, too, classic realist techniques accumulate and multiply to insist with great firmness that Goriot's biography is uniquely the effect of history. By killing his employer, the French Revolution put Goriot in a position to profit from the grain shortages to come. By aggravating those shortages, the Revolution made his profit immense. Because his wealth then permitted the marriages desired by his two daughters, every moment in the ascendant phase of

Goriot's life was directly due to the situation of France at the time it was lived.

Goriot's descending phase was just as tightly connected to vast historical movements. Under the Bourbon Restoration, the nonaristocratic source of their wealth became an intolerable embarrassment to Goriot's daughters. In an effort to conceal their newly unacceptable origins, they first forced their father to give up his life in trade, then tried to hide his existence altogether by refusing to let him be seen with them. Elevated by the Revolution, Goriot was abased by its aftermath. Rastignac's discoveries about his neighbor's biography perfectly exemplify the realist commitment to continuously displaying interpenetration of the collective and the individual.

Several factors thus combine to accord special generic importance to the duchesse de Langeais's speech to Rastignac. *Le Père Goriot*, which is practically a one-volume illustration of the realist aesthetic, grounds itself in the knowledge Rastignac begins to acquire by listening to that speech. Furthermore, Rastignac's instruction is organized around the fundamental insight into human existence in society that Lukács and Auerbach have brilliantly situated at the core of French realism. As a model of the texture of realist prose, the duchesse de Langeais's speech should—if this book's argument is valid—also be a model of realist preference for constative over referential expression.

This preference is not only manifest but takes the arresting form of dissolving all referential authority attributed to the quintessential form of verbal reference, a proper name. In telling Goriot's story, Mme de Langeais calls him indifferently Loriot, Foriot, Doriot, Moriot, and Goriot. Her reaction to Rastignac's insistence on the proper name's proper form is a paradigm for her entire speech.

"I seem to recall that this Foriot . . . "
"Goriot, Madame."
"Yes, this Moriot was president of his section during the Revolution." [90]

The man whose existence should in theory solidify his linguistic designation disappears as his name becomes not a sign attached to a referent but a word spinning off multiple variants on its own indeterminacy. In recounting the biography of a person destroyed by history, Mme de Langeais makes history destroy the word that gave him identity as well. Where there was an individual and a verbal specification of his individuality, there is now an absence fortuitously coupled to verbal slippage. Rastignac's (and the reader's) initiation into the truth of Goriot is an imperious demonstration that Loriot, Moriot, Doriot, and Foriot do not allow truth to impede their exuberant play.

The referential is the language of objective reality, the constative that of social conventions. Mme de Langeais's annihilation of "Goriot" is a compelling display of the priority of conventions over reality in determining the shape of realist communication. Goriot's existence is of no value in stabilizing his identification because the dominant ideology has decreed that his existence no longer counts. As a constative term, "Goriot" is subject to Austin's Rule A.1, that there must exist a conventional procedure having conventional effect for words to do things. Since conventional procedures under the Restoration were not those of the Revolution, "Goriot" does not name a human being but detonates consonantal fission. Like the words of Louis XVI when the National Assembly refused his decree of abolition, the name of Goriot was an empty noise because historical conditions had abolished its referential authority. When "the present king of France" regained its denotational force, "Goriot" became a denotational nightmare.

The character of the historical conditions evacuating the proper name is apparent in two other elements of Mme de Langeais's speech, her double reference to Goriot as an old Ninety-three, "ce vieux Quatre-vingt-treize," and her designation of Napoleon as "Buonaparte" (91). The latter, pronounced as the Italian words *buona parte* (or, for the absolute legitimists, *buon a parte*) and the form of the emperor's name preferred by Restoration notables, is a striking instance of play with a signifier undermining a referent. Besides refusing to accord Napoleon the royal and imperial privilege of designation by his given name, the surname "Buonaparte" denied that the emperor of the French was even French. Like Doriot and Moriot, *Buonaparte* has the characteristically constative power of transferring words' sense from the nature of their referents to the ideology of their users.

"Quatre-vingt-treize," Mme de Langeais's most thorough deformation of "Goriot," simultaneously situates ideology in its historical matrix and defines its constative effect. Referentially an allusion to the Revolution's bloodiest year, Mme de Langeais's "Quatre-vingt-treize" is nevertheless taken away from a year to be applied to a man. What actually happened during the year is irrelevant to the meaning of its name, which comes from the set of ideologically molded procedures allowing it to produce a conventional effect. The referent can shift from a unit of time to a person because referential dependability is irrelevant to constative validity. In Balzac's realist discourse, the sentence "so the heart of that poor Ninety-three bled" (91) is not a variant on the surrealist game of *cadavre exquis* but a demonstration that even piteous human suffering cannot prevent lexical drift. For a constative vision of the world, any set of phonemes can substitute for any other so long as conventional agreements recognize the substitution's legitimacy.

Goriot-Moriot-Foriot-Doriot-Loriot-Quatre-vingt-treize: no name is more authoritative than any other because each expresses the vision of the namer instead of the existence of the named. So dramatic a shift in the verbal function of a proper noun, coming in a passage so crucial to the development of realist fiction, acquires even greater moment because of the strong associations between conventional views of proper nouns and conventional views of realist discourse. As theorists of language from the Greeks to Derrida have pointed out, proper nouns are in important and persuasive ways the best evidence for the thesis that the function of words is to designate things that are not words. Whereas the truth value of a sentence such as "This is a man" depends at least in part on the purely conventional agreements defining the word "man," that of "This is Jean-Joachim Goriot" ought to admit no such ambiguity. Like all other proper nouns, "Jean-Joachim Goriot" has not a definition but a referent, and the intraverbal problematics of words with definitions should not in theory apply to it.

In the duchesse de Langeais's speech, however, the proper noun inaugurates a series of transmutations that confound efforts to protect any verbal category from the metonymic phantasmagoria of signifiers in eruption. When the firmest of all linguistic units becomes loose and flighty, it is impossible to imagine how realist language could achieve its traditional task of conveying the reality of a world prior to language. Is Goriot Goriot, Moriot, or Quatre-vingt-treize? Was Napoleon the emperor of France or an Italian peasant with a comic name? Simply by virtue of the fact that they can be asked, those questions preclude definitive answers. Their formulation in itself conveys the Austinian thesis that conventions rather than reality define an utterance as true or false.

The proper noun is of course one among many manifestations of a convention with incalculable social consequences, that of paternity. What makes a noun proper is the Name of the Father, and that Name's central contribution to societies' survival has been a dominant theme of European research in the human sciences for the better part of this century. Let Jacques Lacan illustrate: "It is in the *name of the father* that we must recognize the support of the Symbolic function which, from the dawn of history, has identified his person with the figure of the law" (*The Language of the Self*, 41). Furthermore, in common with the referential vision of language in general, the social impact of the Name of the Father depends on its supposed connection to an objective fact, the engendering power of heterosexual intercourse. The duchesse de Langeais's aristocratic contempt for the name of a commoner is also an implicit philosophical argument against the referentiality of names in general.

The antipaternal implications in the "Goriot" slippages are of course accented by the fact that, in a text entitled *Le Père Goriot*, the Name of the Father has been "Goriot" from the moment the reader began to read. That association, reinforced in the vast majority of cases where the word *Goriot* appears, is especially strong during Rastignac's instruction, which began when he asked for information about "un père" and was interrupted before he could specify which father he had in mind (85). In apposition throughout the novel, "le père" and "Goriot" are inextricable when the latter dissolves into nothingness.

The former had actually preceded it, for the principal effect of the "père Goriot" syntagm is to eliminate paternity from the paternal sign that inaugurates it. What happens to "Goriot" on the level of the signifier is prepared and completed by what happens to "père" on the level of the signified: instead of the Name of the Father, the father's name becomes a pejorative insult whose mere utterance is enough to expel Rastignac from the Restaud home forever (75–76). Introduction of the character who bears *the* paternal term specifies that he does so as a sign of his abasement ("a former manufacturer... who let himself be called père Goriot," 15) and time after time the text specifies that Goriot's sobriquet is contemptibly inferior to a simple "monsieur" ("père Goriot, who around this time was respectfully named monsieur Goriot," 26). When Mme de Langeais dismembers the second component of *père Goriot*, she merely does to the father's proper name what the novel has done to his common name from its opening words.

Lacan again: "The primordial Law... is revealed clearly enough as identical to an order of Language. For without kinship nominations, no power is capable of instituting the order of preferences and taboos which bind and weave the yarn of lineage down through succeeding generations" (40). As if in illustration of Lacan's point, other "kinship nominations" join that of fatherhood in bathetic disarray when Rastignac learns Goriot's history from his aristocratic informants. When *père* no longer means *père*, the words for the relationships the Father institutes lose their self-identity as well. Here is Mme de Beauséant on Goriot's daughters: "Her sister is no longer her sister; these two women renounce each other as they renounce their father" (93).

If the text does present kinship terms as equivalent to themselves, it is to display the ignorance of those who believe the equivalency holds. Goriot, "believing his daughters would remain his daughters" (89), makes himself their hapless victim. Kinship terms in *Le Père Goriot* cannot affirm what Lacan calls "the primordial Law" because there is no "order of language" when words' analytic relationship has been destroyed, when A does not equal A, "her sister is no longer her sister," and daughters remain daughters nowhere except in the unbalanced imagination of a pathetic old man.

Even when the paternal lexicon is most insistently exalted, its context just as insistently compromises it. At one point in Rastignac's instruction, Mme de Beauséant accords *father* the anaphoric repetition associated with paeans to the most high: "yes, their father, the father, a father, a good father" (89). The occasion for this exuberance, however, is a sentence that denies the devotion attached to the name the vicomtesse so devoutly repeats, Rastignac's "they renounced their father!" Analogously, when Rastignac returns from Mme de Beauséant's to Mme Vauquer's, he expresses his new admiration for Goriot in a sentence that seems to resituate the Name of the Father and other kinship nominations in their rightful place: "Ah! my good neighbor, I am still a son and brother as you are a father" (100). Given that the occasion of Rastignac's feeling of filial and fraternal smugness is that he has just written letters designed to wrench from his family more money than they can afford to give him, however, his "son and brother" are as dizzying as any other kinship term. "I am a son and brother as you are a father" does not correct but highlights the catastrophic uncertainty of fatherhood throughout Balzac's text.

A last example, one deserving its final position: also on his return to the Vauquer pension, Rastignac learns the result of Bianchon's phrenological examination of Goriot's skull. In Bianchon's words, "I tested his head, there's a single bump, the one for paternity, we've got an *Eternal* Father" (97; Balzac's emphasis). God the Father enters the text, capital letters and all, as yet another name for Goriot-Doriot-Moriot-Loriot-Quatre-vingt-treize. Whether manifested on earth or in heaven, the Name of the Father is in *Le Père Goriot* a word that cannot stand still long enough to mean something.

Lacan, Barthes, Claude Lévi-Strauss, and the other French thinkers who have emphasized the contribution of the paternal function to successfully organizing social existence have an immense body of social theory from which to take proofs of their point. Phallocentric conceptualization of the human condition is a venerable tradition, one that acquired special prominence during the Restoration's militant struggle against the Revolution. The idea of the king as father of the French, tirelessly reiterated during and after the Bourbons' return, was so ideologically persuasive a point because it suggested that the Revolution had been a crime against Nature rather than an insurrection against a regime. In conservative thought, the Revolution did not overthrow a political system but attacked the order of the world, the order manifest in the indubitably universal and eternal institution of the family.

Paternal dissolution in *Le Père Goriot* is consequently a game with deadly implications, for the Name of the Father was associated, explicitly and interminably, with the survival of the state. Among the sociopolitical thinkers who illustrate this equation, Louis-Gabriel-Amboise, vicomte de Bonald, deserves special mention. Besides publishing many thousands of pages to repeat that the family units *father, mother, child* are and must be the ground for the social units *power, minister, subject*, Bonald was unfailingly aware that none of these units could preserve themselves if the words for them were subject to historical or cultural alteration: if the Father is to rule, his Name must not vary.

The following passage is from an essay Bonald entitled "De l'origine du langage" in which he argued that language could not have developed and changed through the ages because its original and endless perfection is necessary to express the original and endless perfection of the social order.

> Society was in its beginnings, as it will be until its final days, composed of three *necessary persons, father, mother, child*, or, to generalize these persons and their names so that they refer to public society, *power, minister, subject*. ... Society was therefore complete or *finished* in its beginnings. ... Thus society was in no way able to form language; rather language, the expression of society, necessarily had to be, in its beginnings, complete or finished like society. [VIII, 154–55; my translation]

In view of the deconstructive points that have been made about writing in recent decades, it is worth noting parenthetically that Bonald extends this argument in a companion essay entitled "De l'origine de l'écriture." Like spoken language, writing was for Bonald complete and perfect at its origin, for only thus could the perfection of society be codified and preserved. *Ecriture,* for recent critics the essence of antireferential autonomy, was for the vicomte de Bonald the essence of referential authority, that which showed its majesty at its birth "by fixing and making forever unchangeable the text of the divine laws, fundamental and primitive" (VIII, 262).

Bonald's straightforward identification of the stability of language with that of society and of both with the sovereign position of the Father suggests momentous consequences in the duchesse de Langeais's wayward consonants and the textual play they recapitulate. At issue is the underpinning of Restoration ideology, the natural justification of the social hierarchy inherited from the past. In a book that made assimilation of the natural and the social its founding gesture by taking as its title *Analytical Essay on the Natural Laws of the Social Order,* Bonald identified the contemporary equivalents of *father, mother, child* as *royalty, nobility, Third Estate* (I, 7–8 and passim). This identification, prepared by the announcement that a revolution was going to end (I, 2), makes destruction of the Name of the Father intolerably seditious. Madame de Langeais's deformation of Goriot the name, like textual denigration of Goriot the father, can without strain be understood as contesting the Restoration's survival as a social and political order.

Yet Mme de Langeais's corruption of the Name of the Father is not a diegetic variant of the famous authorial paradox which Marxist critics from Engels to the present have associated with Balzac. Unlike her creator, this aristocratic character falls short of condemning the ideology she wants to defend. For—unlike the vicomte de Bonald—she seems to sense that the natural and the social coincide only when society determines that Nature counts. Although the same natural fact of procreation naming Goriot also names the duchesse de Langeais, she herself is in no danger of becoming Gangeais-Dangeais-Mangeais-Fangeais. In the case of her name, language is what Bonald considered it, a rock-solid articulation of what was in the beginning, is now, and ever shall be.

It is in fact the Name of the Father that gives Mme de Langeais the right to dismember the father's name. As not just a commoner but a commoner enriched by the Revolution, Goriot represents everything the Restoration understood as a crime against Nature. Dissemination of Goriot's name therefore *corrects* an aberration instead of effecting one, affirms social conventions while scorning objective truth and the verbal stability it requires. This unrelenting assault on the referential leaves the constative intact. "Goriot" is variable because the dominant ideology does not incorporate it, because the conventional procedures including such a name are not pertinent to what Mme de Langeais's community recognizes as the world.

The preceding chapter argued that the abolition of Antithesis which Barthes attributes to *Sarrasine* is at the same time a demonstration that verbal antithesis holds so long as a verbal community accepts it. The contrast between "Goriot" and "madame la duchesse de Langeais" develops the demonstration by instituting an antithesis no conceivable referential semantics can underwrite. Rastignac's inaugural lesson on the patronym's nullity simultaneously manifests the constative's majesty.

Preparation for the lesson was a thorough display of how kinship nominations function without reference to kinship. Rastignac is at Mme de Beauséant's for two reasons, because his aunt believed that the vicomtesse would respond to a letter of introduction and because the Restauds have just kicked him out of their house. Each reason shows that the names for relationships are capable of doing things only when the relations they name allow them to perform. "After shaking the branches of the family tree" in response to her nephew's request for information about "the kinship ties that might still be reattached," Rastignac's aunt Marcillac concludes that Mme de Beauséant would be the least frosty if asked for help (42). What matters is not the kinship nomination but the conventions it elicits. Like "Goriot," "Rastignac" and "Marcillac" name only what their listeners determine.

Thanks to Mme de Beauséant's graciousness, Rastignac is admitted to the Restaud household: "By calling himself madame de Beauséant's cousin, he received an invitation from that woman" (44). Note the typically constative form Rastignac's activity takes. It is "by calling himself" an aristocrat that he obtains his invitation, extended so that his hostess will be able to perform the same kind of gratifying speech act as her guest. Mme de Restaud uses the presence of Mme de Beauséant's cousin to invoke the conventional procedure of aristocratic denomination and produces a constative exemplum. Monsieur de Restaud and Maxime de Trailles look at Eugène with undisguised and unbearable contempt until Mme de Restaud makes this introduction.

> "This gentleman," she went on, introducing Eugène to the comte de Restaud, "is monsieur de Rastignac, who is related to madame la vicomtesse de Beauséant through the Marcillac family; I had the pleasure of seeing him at her last ball."
>
> *Related to madame la vicomtesse de Beauséant through the Marcillac family*: these words, spoken almost emphatically by the countess . . . had a magical effect; the count abandoned his coldly ceremonial manner and greeted the student. . . .
>
> Even Comte Maxime de Trailles looked at Eugène with concern and suddenly abandoned his impertinent manner. This wave of the sorcerer's wand (*ce coup de baguette*), due to the powerful intervention of a name, opened new sections in the Southerner's brain and brought back all the witty things he had meant to say. A sudden light let him see clearly in the atmosphere of Parisian society, still shadowy for him. [72]

"Magical effect . . . the sorcerer's wand . . . the powerful intervention of a name . . . see clearly in the atmosphere of Parisian society": such expressions are in accord with Austin's dual conviction that the things words do are wonderful and

93

that the wonders are created by the words' users. Like a magic wand, identification of Eugène's family alters the nature of the world and produces a man where there was a void. Like the performance of a marriage, this metamorphosis occurs only because the formula that produces it figures in one of the conventional procedures by which a collectivity organizes itself. Eugène simultaneously becomes somebody and understands how society functions because both changes depend on a single set of rules.

The irrelevance of facts to application of those rules becomes apparent when Eugène asks his hosts about Goriot. What speech does remains magic, but its power is now destructive rather than creative. The man produced by one set of words is annihilated by another. "In pronouncing the name of père Goriot, Eugène had waved a magic wand (*avait donné un coup de baguette magique*), but this time the effect was the opposite of that produced by these words: related to madame de Beauséant" (76). The striking aspect of the power to negate in Eugène's "père Goriot" is that the kinship those words invoke is incomparably more solid than that underlying the power to produce in "related to madame de Beauséant." Mme de Restaud should not need to "shake the branches of the family tree" to learn that she is related to her father. At issue, however, are conventions rather than facts, constative authority rather than objective accuracy. Because Restoration norms preclude a countess with a plebeian father, the name of the comtesse de Restaud's father must disappear from the discourse in which she figures. Banishment is Eugène's punishment for using referential speech in a setting from which reference is excluded.

Madame de Beauséant, when Eugène first names his relationship to her, reiterates the exclusion. After thinking of his hostess as "my cousin" (79), the provincial visitor puts the thought into words, to devastating effect.

"Cousin," responded Eugène.
"What!" said the vicomesse, flashing a look of freezing contempt at him.

Eugène understood her "What." He had learned so many things
in three hours that he was on the alert. [83]

The most important thing Eugène has learned is that words'
factuality is irrelevant to their nominative function. If he is Mme
de Beauséant's cousin, it is due not to blood but to sufferance,
not to his family but to his interlocutor. A mood change is
enough to convert the vicomtesse's "What!" into "Well now,
cousin" (84) and to have her introduce Mme de Langeais to
"monsieur de Rastignac, a cousin of mine" (85). The narrative
voice subsequently ratifies this introduction by describing Mme
de Beauséant's reaction to "her cousin" (88). The degree of
kinship in kinship nominations has nothing to do with a fact,
everything to do with an attitude.

Like "père" and "Goriot," therefore, "cousin" undergoes the
same metonymic fission that Barthes found in *Sarrasine*. And,
like *Sarrasine*, *Le Père Goriot* suggests in a multitude of ways
that words' capacity for fission does not in the least affect their
solidity when society has something for them to do. Instead of
endlessly proliferating, the metonymy is rigorously controlled
in a clear illustration of why Wittgenstein contended that at any
given moment there is indeed a last house on the road. When
Mme de Beauséant formally recognizes Eugène as her cousin in
the paradigmatically performative sentence "I give you my
name" (94), his identity becomes as firm as Goriot's is shaky.
The rest of the novel (like much of the rest of *La Comédie
humaine*) shows him capitalizing on a kinship term whose power
is undiminished by previous insistence on its referential undecidability. In theaters and concert halls, at balls and receptions,
in the aristocratic faubourg Saint-Germain and the bourgeois
chaussée d'Antin, Mme de Beauséant's fellows and imitators
perpetuate the truth of Rastignac's relationship to her. "He had
a status in society by virtue of being the recognized cousin of
madame de Beauséant" (170–71), and his position is no less
real for depending not on the descriptive accuracy of *cousin* but
on the constative authority of *recognized*.

Cousin therefore joins all the text's other kinship nominations as a word that does things in conformity with Austin's argument that collective conventions are the sole ground for the things done. The precise degree of Rastignac's relationship to Mme de Beauséant is immaterial, for blood determines his social position no more than it establishes Goriot's paternity. If *cousin* works while *père* becomes an insult, if "Rastignac" names a force while "Goriot" quivers and dissipates, the reason is a collectively accepted protocol rather than a referentially established difference. The names that count in *Le Père Goriot* are constative affirmations of social position, and the defining trait of all constative affirmations is their dissociation from objective reality.

The realist constative has emptiness at its core but solidity on its surface, and Rastignac is acutely aware that the solidity of his own identity requires a great deal of money. When Vautrin jokingly calls him "monsieur le marquis," Rastignac's response is angry but perceptive. "Here, to be a real marquis, you've got to have a hundred-thousand-livre income" (96). In Rastignac's mind, a real marquis is the product not of the familial origin that ought to confer the title but of enough money to buy the things with which the title is associated. Those things elicit the appropriate social response, and social response constitutes the entirety of constative identity. Really to be a marquis means not having the right father but displaying the right signs.

On acquiring what he considers a sufficient amount of money, Rastignac undergoes an inner as well as an outer transformation. The strong phallic overtones in description of what money does to Rastignac are a powerful indication of what is at stake in any such conversion. "The instant money slips into a student's pocket, there is erected in him a fantastic column that is his support.... Unheard of phenomena take place in him, he wants to do everything and can do everything.... All Paris belongs to him" (112). The corollary is obvious. Without money, there is no fantastic column and hence no phallic identity. Madame de Beauséant took only a first step when she gave Eugène her name and allowed him to be her cousin. "Really" to bear such a kinship nomination requires money as well as indulgence, and Vautrin is correct when he points out over and over that money is what Eugène lacks. In *Sarrasine*, the mysterious figure in the

Lanty household is a man because money gives him the right
to be what he chooses. In *Le Père Goriot*, Eugène's poverty
constrains him to struggle endlessly in order to retain the aristocratic position to which his birth in theory entitles him.

In both cases, money and identity combine in a univocal
statement of constative truth, for the money Eugène must have
is not that which buys things but that which establishes position.
Or, more accurately, the things money buys are not objects but
signs, conventional features of a conventional procedure that
functions in exactly the same way as such verbal sequences as
"related to madame la vicomtesse de Beauséant through the
Marcillac family." The hundred-thousand-franc income Rastignac believes necessary for a real marquis is essential because
the things bought on such an income are immediately *interpreted*. They signify by virtue of their position in a clear semiotic
structure. Their constitutive function in producing status derives
from their capacity to elicit determinate hermeneutic operations
from those before and for whom they are displayed.

Identifying money as the pivot around which the Balzacian
universe revolves is of course hardly a new insight. A huge and
powerful body of criticism, Marxist and non-Marxist, has demonstrated money's centrality to the characters, plots, and style
of the *Comédie humaine*. The contribution of a speech-act perspective is not to show that money talks in Balzac but to heighten
attention to what it says. Riches are needed to sustain a social
role, to be a real marquis, to be what one is supposed to be
even without money. According to Restoration ideology, an
objective event, the fact of birth, creates the identity that social
discourse incorporates into its naming procedures. By repeatedly
showing that birth is not pertinent to identity, Balzacian insistence on money widens the gap between social discourse and
objective facts. Besides condemning him to hunger, Goriot's
poverty also makes him something other than a father. Besides
clothing him, Rastignac's wealth makes him Rastignac. The
things money buys are the significant features of an insistently
constative language.

On his expulsion from the Restaud home, Rastignac lists the
objects he needs in order to remain in Parisian society. That he

is also cataloging semiotic units is evident in the list's conclusion, a vulgar outburst against Goriot and the negative impact of his name. "Can I go out into society when, to get around properly, I need a heap of carriages, polished boots, indispensable trinkets, gold chains, white kid gloves that cost six francs for the mornings and countless yellow gloves for the evenings? Silly old père Goriot!" (77). What leads from gloves, boots, carriages, and golden chains to Goriot, from commodities to a name? It is the common status of the commodities and the name as incantatory formulas given power by the collective response they evoke. To counteract the effect of a name, Rastignac needs things, and his associative processes are puzzling only if we mistakenly assume that things and names are qualitatively distinct. As a sign was responsible for his expulsion from a social milieu, so signs can effect his reintegration. The imperative to be wealthy comes from the social hermeneutics attendant on display of wealth.

Vautrin understands this perfectly. As he explains to Rastignac, the actual possession of riches is irrelevant. What matters is that other people assume that riches are possessed: "So if you want to make your fortune fast, you must already be rich, or look like you are (*être déjà riche, ou le paraître*)" (125). The venerable distinction between *être* and *paraître* is now an equation. When statements are constative rather than referential, being and appearing are merged.

The fantastic column that money erects in Rastignac is in direct oppostion to the fantastic void produced in Goriot by lack of money. Phallic identity and phallic dissolution have the same cause, the medium society uses to evaluate the goods circulating within it. The Name of the Father has become the Balance of the Account, and the Father stops being himself when he loses the wherewithal to keep money's circulation active and vigorous. Rastignac needs money to signify his identity as a full member of aristocratic society, Goriot to signify his position as a father. Procreation has no more to do with paternity than with aristocracy, for every social category is the effect of social performance. Goriot's laments that he can no longer be a father because he has no money to give his children furnish the novel's most sustained illustration of fatherhood's absolute prerequisite.

What is the conventional procedure that has the conventional effect of paternity? Goriot's answer is the novel's: to be a father is to participate actively in the socially regulated exchange of goods. "Fathers must always give in order to be happy. Always giving is what makes you a father" (235); "I'm not good for anything now, I'm not a father anymore! No! She's asking me, she needs something! And I'm a poor wretch who doesn't have anything" (262); "Money is life. It does everything" (252). Those and countless comparable outbursts convey a single message. Because giving makes one a father, not giving makes one something else. Far from the natural result of an objective fact, fatherhood is in *Le Père Goriot* a fortuitous intersection in the supremely unnatural process of monetary circulation.

When he learns that his daughter Anastasie is being forced to surrender control of her fortune to her husband, Goriot vows to prevent so monstrous a transgression by kidnapping the Restauds' oldest son. This criminal project is envisioned in terms reminiscent of those with which Rastignac conceptualizes aristocracy. Whether the goal is to be a real father or a real marquis, money is essential to achieving it.

> "Nasie, you can rest easy. Oh, so he cares about his heir! Good, good. I'll take his son who, blast it all, is my grandson. I've got a right to see the kid, I suppose? I'll put him in my village. I'll take care of him, don't worry about that. I'll make him surrender, the monster, by telling him, 'The fight's on! If you want your son back, give her property back to my daughter and let her do what she wants.' "
> "My father!"
> "Yes, your father! Ah, I'm a real father." [258]

For Goriot—"he cares about his *heir*"—monsieur de Restaud is vulnerable not because he loves his son but because he needs a person to whom his money will be conveyed. Goriot claims the right to kidnap that person because his own paternity is threatened by his daughter's loss of the money he gave her. In both families, the father is "real" only if he transmits money to his child. In Goriot's apostrophe to M. de Restaud, "If you want

your son back, give her property back to my daughter," *son,*
daughter, and *property* are lexically as well as pragmatically
substitutes for one another in a system of kinship nominations
completely dissociated from birth. If they are to remain fathers,
Goriot must retrieve Anastasie's wealth and Restaud must preserve his heir. The kidnapping scenario sees one father as having
money but no child and the other as having a child but no
money. Neither condition is "real" paternity because neither
permits the socioeconomic activity on which paternity depends.

A constative vision of the paternal function also animates *Le
Père Goriot*'s crucial subplot, which concludes when Victorine
Taillefer's father officially recognizes that she is his daughter.
Referentially, Victorine's familial situation is never in doubt. In
Mme de Couture's words, father and daughter are physically
so alike that their relationship is self-evident to whoever sees
them together. "I don't know how he can deny she's his, she
looks exactly like him" (61). Referential facts do not count,
however, for M. Taillefer refuses the constative act of naming
Victorine his child. "Without saying his daughter" (61), he
leaves Victorine in an unbearable limbo where her name and
family are not hers.

When Vautrin's scheme for killing M. Taillefer's son succeeds,
Victorine's referential condition remains the same but her constative identity is transmuted. Her father calls her his daughter,
and the name she acquires produces a radically different existence. "Her father is forced to adopt her" (215) for the same
reason M. de Restaud would have to return Anastasie's money
if Goriot carried out his kidnapping, because fathers cannot be
fathers unless they transmit funds to their children.

Vautrin said as much when he originally outlined his Taillefer
scheme to Rastignac. "Père Taillefer . . . has an only son he wants
to leave his property to, at Victorine's expense. . . . If God's will
were to take his son from him, Taillefer would welcome his
daughter back; he'd want an heir of some kind—a stupid but
natural desire—and I know he can't have any more children"
(129).

As with the Restauds, so with the Taillefers: "child" is another
word for "heir." The act by which M. Taillefer recognizes Vic-

torine is the consequence of the paternal imperative to assure that money reaches its intended recipient. He undertakes the performative process of making Victorine his daughter (recall the curious sentence "her *father* is forced to *adopt* her") so that he can continue to perform his own identity as a socially recognized father.

Fatherhood's definition as a convention not a condition receives its most poignant formulation during Goriot's death agony. The dying man realizes that his children were his children and he their father only because speech acts performed the relationship, because "they *said* they were my daughters, and they *recognized* me as their father" (290; my emphasis). It is as Mme de Beauséant's "recognized cousin" that Rastignac becomes a force, and it is for lack of the same recognition that Goriot becomes a void. As the creation of a conventional procedure, identity cannot survive the procedure's withdrawal.

Goriot's dying vision of the wonders of devotion that would be worked around his deathbed if he were still rich is his understanding that paternity is never performed except according to the protocols accepted by society. "Oh, if I were rich, if I had kept my fortune, if I hadn't given it to them, they'd be here, they'd keep my cheeks wet with their kisses! I'd be living in a huge house, I'd have beautiful rooms, servants, my own fire, and they'd be all teary, with their husbands and their children. I'd have all that. But nothing. Money gives everything, even daughters" (289).

This passage is something besides another textual condemnation of the venal Parisian world in which the most sacred human obligations are ignored if they offer no financial gain. Negative moral commentary takes the form of affirmative financial vision. If poverty takes children away, wealth produces them: "Money gives everything, even daughters." The man whose paternity is unverifiable would with money be a man whose paternity is constantly enacted by children and grandchildren following every convention of filial love and devotion, all of them eager to plant their adoring kisses on their father's cheek.

In a supremely laconic sentence—"But nothing"—Goriot describes what paternity actually is. With much more expansive rhetoric, he describes what it would be if he had kept his money. Although the final section of *Le Père Goriot* is entitled "The Death of the Father," what dies is only the referential concept of fatherhood. The constative definition remains authoritative, as Goriot unknowingly demonstrates in maxims that validate paternity as a convention while destroying it as an absolute. "A father must always be rich" (289–90); or "Il faut toujours se faire valoir" (293). *Se faire valoir* has the ambiguity that Barbara Johnson points out in the key Austinian terms *perform* and *act* (*Critical Difference*, 65). All three verbs simultaneously signify something real and something false, all refer at the same time to a fact and its imitation. Goriot's death agony is a long meditation on the irresoluble duality of *se faire valoir*. While ceasing to mean anything in itself, fatherhood retains the power to mean everything provided the correct conventional procedures are applied. The nothingness in which Goriot dies because he believed the family was a natural unit does not blind him to the plenitude of filial love as a sanctioned social performance.

As the supreme vehicle for collective sanctions, money invigorates paternity with the same demonstrativeness that poverty displays in evacuating it. The dying Goriot remembers as well as fantasizes occupying the father's place. "So when some of those sophisticated people whispered in my son-in-law's ear: 'Who's that man?' 'He's the father with the money, he's rich.' 'The devil you say!' and they looked at me with the respect due the money" (290). Although it was not elicited by paternity, the respect Goriot received when he was rich was solid and real. The paternal word in "father with money" commands homage no less strongly than that in "father without a sou" repels it. Valorized by an attribute society finds worthy, the father and his name are awesome.

The previous chapter addressed Barthes's habit of enclosing words that designate reality in quotation marks. There I argued that the constative real is not what precedes but what succeeds the "real" as spoken and performed. Applied to the dying Goriot, that argument delineates a father without "fatherhood" pleading for the enactment essential to actual existence as a progenitor. Desperately though he wants to believe that paternity is an absolute value needing no establishment, Goriot's comments continually suggest that the paternal principle is nonexistent apart from social enforcement. Because no one can be a father unless he is a "father," any means are legitimate if they lead to the requisite performance. "My daughters, my daughters, Anastasie, Delphine! I want to see them. Send the police to get them, use force! Justice is on my side, everything's on my side, nature, laws! I protest! The country will perish if fathers are trampled under like this. That much is clear. Society, the world depends on fatherhood, everything collapses if children don't love their fathers" (291).

Proof of fatherhood's conventionality is cruel in the conventional methods that this father advocates to bring his children to his deathbed. As an exemplary performative utterance, Goriot's "I protest" invokes the institutional system empowered to recognize protests as legitimate. The father must therefore plead for constative assertion of his paternity in the very process of proclaiming that paternity is a referential absolute requiring no systemic ratification. To be efficacious, this protest must be sustained by the *social* forces whose pertinence to *natural* duties the protest intends to deny. Simply by virtue of the terms in which it is made, Goriot's call for help is an admission of defeat.

The call concludes with a vision of society's utter dissolution. "The country will perish if fathers are trampled under like this. ...Society, the world depends on fatherhood." Those apocalyptic sentences assume a definition of paternity incompatible with a biography showing time and again that what counts is not the Father but the Name. Although society is indeed based on fatherhood, it is also based on the principle that the force of all such foundational words comes not from their reference but from their function. Goriot dies alone because his paternity is a natural fact in a world where social facts are supreme.

The marriage ceremony, one of Austin's original examples of performative speech, is in *Le Père Goriot* one of the clearest demonstrations of fatherhood's conventionality. Every attempt to define the family as natural must elide the fact that all families originate in an artificial ceremony varying with the norms of the group in which it takes place. Most naturalistic visions of the family obscure the elision. Goriot makes it explicit by crying out that (natural) families can endure only if (conventional) marriages are forbidden. The consequence is a bitter irony. In defense of the family, Goriot pleads that there be no more marriages, which is of course to plead that there be no more families. Nowhere is paternity's constative definition more apparent than in Goriot's absurd demand for prohibition of the convention that legitimates paternity as a value. "Fathers, tell the legislature to pass a law about marriage! In the end, you can't let your daughters marry if you love them. The son-in-law is a scoundrel who spoils everything about a daughter, he makes everything dirty. No more marriages! they take our daughters away from us, and we don't have them when we die. Pass a law about the death of fathers!" (295) The paradox in this appeal for marriages to be outlawed is the same as that in the appeal for children to be made filial. Each assertion of natural duty is addressed to a conventional institution, in this case the legislature. To urge that marriage be outlawed is to admit that the paternity that marriage authorizes is also subject to repeal. Goriot's "No more marriages!" demands at one and the same time that he be respected as a father and that the social practice making fatherhood respectable be abolished. In the terms of Austin's Rule A.1, Goriot has the impossible desire to eliminate a conventional procedure while keeping its conventional effect whole and pure.

In Goriot's view, his sons-in-law destroyed his position as a father by taking away his daughters. But his daughters' alienation simply confirms that the family is not a given but a creation, not the will of God but the custom of a community. As only constative speech can express the effects of a communal custom, Goriot's exaltation of *father* and denigration of *son-in-law* is a hysterical misapprehension. The word *son-in-law* is unmistakably the product of a conventional procedure; it proclaims what the word *father* obscures, that there is no family apart from social validation of the names for its members. To become a father, one does something; to become a son-in-law, one says something. The distinction is objectively real but practically inconsequential, for neither what is done nor what is said signifies in and of itself. Acts and words alike acquire semantic content only within a social matrix, and within Goriot's social matrix procreation is value-free.

Goriot's dying plea that marriage be outlawed is prompted by the same concepts that produced Austin's inaugural suggestion that marriage be carefully contemplated. For both men, marriage is a clear demonstration that human existence and the words expressing its nature are a matter of pure convention. For Austin, the demonstration was the underpinning for a philosophical system. For Goriot, it was fatal refutation of the belief that some things stand independently of the forms in which a collectivity represents them.

Marriage and the son-in-law reveal society's actual structure for Mme de Langeais as well. While telling Rastignac about Goriot's past life, the dutchess defines the "drama of the son-in-law" as a central motif of their decadent world.

> "Heavens," said madame de Langeais, "yes, that seems quite horrible, and yet we see it every day. Isn't there a reason? Tell me, my dear, have you ever thought about what a son-in-law is? He's a man for whom the two of us will raise a dear little creature bound to us in a thousand ways, who will for seventeen years be the joy of the family, what Lamartine would call its white soul, and who will become its plague. . . . I hear people ask what there is dramatic in society today; but the drama of the son-in-law is frightful, not to mention our marriages, which have become really stupid things." [90]

Mme de Langeais's statement that marriage transforms the family's "soul" into its "plague" invites development. The soul gives life, the plague death. When marriage dissolves the thousand bonds keeping the daughter in her place, therefore, the family comes to an end. Yet that end is also a beginning, for one family's death is another's birth. Mme de Langeais bumps into the same quandary as Goriot. Every father must begin as a son-in-law if he is to deserve the paternal name; the son-in-law unseating the father perpetuates his position. There are contradictory answers to Mme de Langeais's "have you ever thought about what a son-in-law is?" If a daughter's marriage destroys the family, it also creates it, and neither the negative nor the positive function is conceivable without the other.

Because a family that already exists must be dissolved for another family to come to be, no family can lay claim to irrevocable integrity. The actual horror of the son-in-law is that, by exposing the family as a conventional effect, he reveals the conventional base of existence as a whole. "The drama of the son-in-law is frightful" because it suggests that the Name of the Father is nothing more than the effect of a ceremony. Madame de Langeais implies as much by defining the family as a performance, as a "drama" in which roles are assumed and can thus be abandoned. "What there is dramatic in society today" is everything in society today, an agglomeration of identities that hold only so long as they are enacted.

Mme de Langeais's insistent repetition of "drama" recalls the lexical imperative concerning that word in the first paragraph of *Le Père Goriot*: "It is necessary to use the word drama here" (5). This necessity rapidly produces a sentence containing five occurrences of the word to characterize Mme Vauquer's boarders. "These boarders induced presentments of completed or ongoing dramas; not those dramas played before footlights and painted canvas but living, mute dramas, frozen dramas that stirred the heart to warmth, continuous dramas" (18). Although the principal purpose of *drama* in that sentence is to make the common Balzacian announcement that a pending narrative is fascinating and momentous, the word's theatrical sense is crucial. *Le Père Goriot* is a constant equivocation between different kinds of dramatic performance, those that have artificial trappings and those that are lived. The Vauquer pension is the stage for serial changes of roles culminating in the message that no role can command adherence unless it is well scripted and well played. The apparent oxymoron in "living dramas" vanishes when the novel recapitulates a socially imposed scenario that writes Goriot out with the same authoritative control employed to write Rastignac in.

Immediately after she copies the narrative voice by repetitively foregrounding the word "drama," the duchesse de Langeais starts her dismemberment of the word "Goriot." The transition is effortless because the two operations develop a single concept of lexical validity. Like the drama of the son-in-law, that of the father is a sustained demonstration that language names convincingly only when what it names is coherent social practice.

Among Mme Vauquer's boarders, the man who affirms the performative nature of his identity is the man most comfortable with the performance's result, Vautrin. He alone has taken a name with no natural origin in a father, and he alone states with assurance that his name is a fact: "Who am I? Vautrin" (118). So ringing an affirmation is inconceivable from Goriot-Moriot-Loriot and the other characters at Mme Vauquer's, none of whom shares Vautrin's awareness that signs are arbitrary. In Vautrin's vision of the world, the conventional procedure of bearing a name can be dispensed with altogether if the requisite conventional effect is achieved without it. "If I succeed, nobody will ask 'Who are you?' I'll be monsieur Four-Million" (126).

Vautrin's disregard for the Father is such that he prepares this comical reduction of identity to whatever circulates in society by a double announcement that he will become monsieur Four-Million by leading "the patriarchal life." The patriarch is not he who bears the Name of the Father but he who knows that the Name needs the Father not at all. Again money is the synecdoche for all the means that society employs as evaluative tools, and again positive evaluation in no way entails the actual presence of its supposed cause.

Vautrin, who has "more than ten thousand *brothers*" (225; my emphasis), extends his concept of the Father's arbitrariness to other kinship nominations as well. His paternal solicitude for Eugène produces an adoption procedure including this succinct lesson on social truth: "There are no principles, there are only events; there are no laws, there are only circumstances" (130). In Austinian terms, there are no facts, there are only conventions. The contrast between "Vautrin" and "Goriot" is between a name that is explicitly a sign and a name pretending to adhere to a reality. The latter's dissipation encapsulates the text's lessons on the gulf between referential accuracy and constative validity.

Banal though it is to address Rastignac's situation between the two father figures "père Goriot" and "papa Vautrin," the contrast between the proper names "Goriot" and "Vautrin" prompts comparison of the paternal words "père" and "papa." "Père" is the father in his majesty, the word taken by all those who occupy the exalted paternal position from God through the king to a peasant providing a hut for his family. "Papa" is a familiar colloquialism, a spoken term that expresses an attitude rather than a position, a relationship rather than an autonomy. To appreciate the difference, imagine Lacan and other recent theorists expounding on the sociopsychological ramifications of "le nom du papa" instead of "le nom du père."

That so childish a term as *papa* cannot convey the weighty messages attached to *père* was obvious to Pierre Larousse. The article "papa" in the *Grand dictionnaire universel* distinguishes "Aryan" languages from those heard "among the Negroes of Africa" in part by pointing out that in European speech *papa* and *maman* "are heard exclusively in children's speech." Advanced civilizations require an advanced term to name the paternal function, and *papa* just does not measure up.

Yet it is *père* that collapses in *Le Père Goriot*, a failure defining Rastignac's filial options as a choice between reference and solidity. "Goriot" and "père" have firm existential reality behind them and nevertheless they evaporate. "Vautrin" and "papa" are oral performances without referential claims, yet their impact on Eugène is decisive. Like the distinction between *gendre* and *père*, that between "Goriot" and "Vautrin" inexorably demonstrates that meaning is a conventional effect best produced when words openly accept that their only reference is to what they themselves do.

Eugène's performance will not, however, replicate Vautrin's. The difference comes to the fore in Rastignac's deformation of Vautrin's statement on the options available to any member of a social group, which is to say to any human being. In his own view, Vautrin speaks "with the superiority of a man who, after examining things here below, saw that there were only two courses to take: either dumb obedience or revolt" (119). Later, after Vautrin's arrest and the onset of Goriot's fatal illness, Rastignac converts his mentor's dyad into a triplet. "He had seen the three great expressions of society: Obedience, Struggle, and Revolt; the Family, Paris (*le monde*), and Vautrin" (276). The choice between acceptance and revolt has acquired a third term, struggle against society but by its rules. That is the course Rastignac takes, and his progress on it is a sustained illustration of the realist constative in operation.

Rastignac personifies the two-term schema of obedience and revolt as the family and Vautrin, as the father and the criminal. The former embodies meaning as a referential derivation, the latter as a creative poetics. Vautrin's name is what he makes it, but by making it without attending to social rules he risks losing it. His arrest and unmasking are a debaptism in which society reasserts the supremacy of its own procedures for identifying its members. In Vautrin's case, socially enacted identification even has the material, corporeal form of the convict's "T.F." brand on his shoulder. As it erases the name Goriot was born to, so society erases the name Vautrin came to. Neither objective reality nor individual creativity stands against a collectivity's will to insure that its conventions have their prescribed effect.

Rastignac's consciousness of the power inherent in the collective will is apparent when he defines Obedience, Struggle, and Revolt as "the three great expressions of society." Even revolt against it is one of society's expressions of itself. Despite its awesome grandeur, Vautrin's resolution to withhold obedience does not provide an escape from the dominion of communal practices. The name he took for himself is in a series with two supremely social entities, the family and Parisian society, as so many articulations of a transcendent whole no part of which can violate the protocols keeping the whole together. The name "Vautrin" disappears because it threatened the laws of social cohesion.

Rastignac ultimately determines that the same fate will not overtake "Rastignac," a sign that will be ratified by all the procedures requisite for it to have effect. Unlike Vautrin, Rastignac obtained his name through a process recognized as valid by his fellows. Unlike Goriot, Rastignac behaves as though aware that recognition of validity does not proceed automatically from the facts it claims to endorse. The man who conquers society as "the recognized cousin of madame de Beauséant" is the man who understands that the road to conquest has already been laid out for him.

The paternal names "Goriot" and "Vautrin" are complementary violations of constative protocols. Based on reference alone, "Goriot" vanishes when society shows that reference is not pertinent to identity. Based on individual prowess alone, "Vautrin" vanishes when society reaffirms the principle that individuals are not to be confused with monads. "Rastignac" survives because it confirms the community's right to name without implying that the ground for such a right must lie outside the community exercising it. The third term Rastignac adds to Vautrin's dyad is less a middle way than a dialectical transcendence. Obedience and Revolt come together in Struggle, which combines the former's acceptance of social rules with the latter's conviction that the rules need no objective validity.

Considered in relation to verbal reference and verbal play, the realist constative is the same kind of dialectical transcendence. It too recognizes the arbitrariness of social expression without positing a space beyond the constraints imposed by society's need to express. The family, *le monde*, and Vautrin: in its indeterminate senses of "world" and "society"—of the whole and the part—the central term *monde* powerfully conveys the text's vision of an all-inclusive conventionality. What society performs *is* the world for its members, and no good comes of contemplating facts not collectively recognized as factual.

Just after his meditation on society's three great expressions, Rastignac turns his thoughts to the family's apparent insulation from the society it also expresses. "In his thoughts he was borne back into the bosom of his family. He recalled the pure emotions of that calm life, remembered the days he spent surrounded by those who cherished him. Conforming to the natural laws of the domestic hearth, those dear creatures found a full, unbroken happiness, without anxieties" (276). For my purposes, two factors are crucial in this pastoral interruption of Rastignac's social education. First, the family is defined as a natural rather than a created institution, and its *natural* laws promise endless contentment to all who obey them. Second (as is so often the case with pastoral escapes), Rastignac unhesitatingly refuses the perfect life offered by obeying natural laws. The full, unbroken happiness without anxieties is spurned, for Rastignac's vision of familial bliss leads directly to his decision to profane the family by ignoring Delphine's duty to her dying father in order to take her to the Beauséant ball. The family is everything society is not, but what is not society can appeal only to the imagination. In terms of their narrative impact, the pure joys of familial contentment are as hollow as the paternal vocabulary in the syntagm "père Goriot." Without practical consequence of any kind, Rastignac's idyllic vision of family life constitutes at most a formulaic banality.

Family life therefore has great representational value but no constative force. Nothing social contributes the solidity necessary for familial language to ground a being. The same opposition between constative and representational value organizes Eugène's reaction to the death of Goriot, "a being who, for Eugène, *represented* Fatherhood" (305; my emphasis). That quotation comes during an extended textual demonstration that the father's death and the disappearance of his name do not in any way disrupt the normal course of social exchange. Eating, drinking, talking, and joking go on without hindrance from Goriot, who—in the ultimate metonymic spin-off of Loriot-Moriot-Foriot-Doriot-Quatre-vingt-treize—becomes with his dying breath "a little deathorama" (304). The figure who represents Fatherhood with a capital *F* for Eugène is deprived of the constative identity necessary to represent anything whatever to a group larger than one.

And a group much larger than one is Eugène's choice after he buries Goriot and enters the constative universe par excellence, a world in which signification never claims to be anything other than collective performance. Rastignac's Père Lachaise scene—in its memorialization of a Jesuit, the name of the setting is the novel's final display of paternity's irrelevance to the paternal lexicon—continues the development begun by adding Struggle to Vautrin's Obedience or Revolt. In tacit confirmation of that continuity, the defiant "A nous deux" with which Rastignac goes down to Paris repeats the words of those who represent the family and its rejection, père Goriot (258) and papa Vautrin (119). Here too the third term transcendently affirms how collectivities mean, here too the "challenge he hurled at Society" (309) also venerates Society's right to its capital letter. When the novel's closing words recount Rastignac's move from Goriot's grave to Delphine's table, the Father is definitively severed from the conventions organizing social coexistence and validating social nomination.

The unnarrated Nucingen dinner with Goriot fresh in his grave corresponds to the narrated Beauséant ball with Goriot writhing on his deathbed. Both social functions substitute for the paternal function, both ratify Name and Law while the Father dies and decays. The Nucingen dinner obliterates Goriot but begins production of the identity that will eventually make Rastignac a count, a minister, and a peer of France with an annual income of 300,000 francs. The Beauséant ball obliterates Goriot but incorporates Rastignac among Paris notables, transforms Delphine from a woman of no consequence to a woman of substance, and displays Anastasie in the diamonds necessary for her to remain a woman of honor. It is on the Father's dilapidation that the power of the Name is consolidated.

Rastignac senses as much when he considers that the presence of Goriot's daughters at the Beauséant ball entails absence from their dying father's side. On Delphine: "He felt that she was capable of walking on her father's corpse to get to the ball" (276). On Anastasie: " 'She has,' said Rastignac, 'made collateral of her father's death' " (281). The father's corpse, the father's death, the daughters' ball: annihilation of the family's origin is the precondition for its members' denomination by their community. The conventional procedures producing the conventional effect of identity unfold in the absence of the figure that identity theoretically evokes.

Read in the context of the ball during which the Father dies, the dinner following his burial is a postdiegetic suggestion of the process through which the Name circulates. The coincidence of Rastignac's ascent with Goriot's disappearance summarizes the dual thematics of constative identity. Dramatically and definitively separated from the father, the paternal function attaches firmly to society. Without connection to any individual, denomination is inextricable from a collectivity. Rastignac's stellar performance in Restoration Paris begins as one component of a sustained textual argument that success depends on nothing more than skillful manipulation of the conventions a community recognizes as its own.

In their discussion of speech-act theory's unique sensitivity to the interpenetration of verbal performance and social convention, several important figures in recent literary theory have attended more carefully to what conventionality excludes than to what it produces. Since the contention here is that it is precisely the productivity of speech acts that distinguishes constative identity, I want to conclude this discussion of *Le Père Goriot* by contrasting its vision of performative truth to the representations of Austin made by Jacques Derrida, Barbara Johnson, and Stanley Fish.

Derrida comes directly to grips with Austin in "Signature Event Context." While admiring Austin's determined effort to take the philosophy of language out of the dead-end street to which his predecessors had directed it, Derrida is sharply critical of several presuppositions underlying speech-act theory. For Derrida, Austin's most important failure is the decision not to consider a performative utterance if it is "said by an actor on the stage, or if introduced in a poem, or spoken in soliloquy" (Austin, 22). As was stated earlier, for a deconstructionist this exclusion comes close to invalidating the entire Austinian concept of speech, of acts, and of their interaction. Austin's refusal to examine what he calls "non-serious" (122) utterances precludes consideration of the sine qua non of all utterances, their ineluctable citationality and iterability. Austin's performative rests on an axiomatic determination that the very thing making speech possible is not pertinent to speech's performative variety. Derrida asks: "For, finally, is not what Austin excludes as anomalous, exceptional, 'non-serious,' that is, *citation* (on the stage, in a poem, or in a soliloquy), the determined modification of a general citationality—or rather, a general iterability—without which there would not even be a 'successful' performative?" (325) In this analysis, the component of performative language Austin declined to consider is the constitutive core of any kind of language. Speech-act theory, erected as it is on illegitimate constriction of what counts as speech, is condemned to repeat an equally illegitimate vision of the act as a self-present entity immediately definable in its totality.

Austin's decision to ignore performative utterances spoken on stage and in poems is a statement that such a context prevents the words that figure in a standard conventional procedure from having their standard conventional effect. Spoken by an actor playing a role, "We find the defendant guilty of murder in the first degree" leads neither to an execution nor to a prison term. Austin sees this kind of imitative performative as a "parasitic" (22) repetition of the normal and ordinary speech he wants to take as his sole concern.

Derrida's most telling argument is that the normal and ordinary use of the performative must in its turn be a parasitic citation if it is to be effective. Let me retain the example of a murder trial's conclusion. In order for material consequences to follow the utterance finding the defendant guilty, that utterance must itself iterate a preestablished formula already defined as suitable to conclude this kind of judicial proceeding. Conventional effect can come only from a previously patterned conventional procedure that stands as a codified whole without performing any action whatever. How does the jury's foreman know to say "We find the defendant guilty of murder in the first degree" and not "Roses are red, violets are blue, he's guilty as surely as dairy cows moo"? Because the proper formulation is no less citation of a model that precedes it than an actor's repetition of the same formulation on stage. "Could a performative statement succeed if its formulation did not repeat a 'coded' or iterable statement, in other words if the expressions I use to open a meeting, launch a ship or a marriage were not identifiable as *conforming* to an iterable model, and therefore if they were not identifiable in a way as 'citation'?" (326). To Austin's opposition between a real performative and its parasitic imitation, Derrida counters by showing that there can be no real performative that does not parasitically imitate something that is its ineluctable precondition. What Austin excluded from consideration in order to communicate the nature of the performative is the very thing that gives the performative its nature.

"Signature Event Context" has had remarkable and deserved influence on the attitudes toward Austin among contemporary literary scholars. It seems to me certain that Austin's neat contrast between ordinary and parasitic speech acts cannot withstand Derrida's argument for the necessary iterability of all language, including language that is an event.

But the problems identified by Austin do not go away simply because we now recognize the illegitimacy of some of the vocabulary prominent in *How to Do Things with Words*. However firmly we believe that the conclusion of a trial for murder in a play cannot be opposed term by term to the same conclusion in a courtroom, we must still deal with the fact that *some* form of opposition remains. Although the words they hear are equally citational, the lives of the courtroom and stage defendant are affected in ways that do not overlap. Misguided though it was for Austin to define such repetitive utterances as unassimilable, it remains certain that their effects are far from indistinguishable.

When Derrida subjects all performatives to the condition he calls iterability, he does not pretend to abolish the special characteristics of words that actually do things, for example, perform a marriage or convict a defendant. "Not that citationality here is of the same type as in a play, a philosophical reference, or the recitation of a poem. That is why there is a relative specificity, as Austin says, a 'relative purity' of performatives" (326). Despite such admissions of the performative's relative specificity, however, Derrida's principal concern is to show that the specificity cannot be absolute. All statements that something distinguishes verbal performance of, say, a marriage from an openly identified imitation of that performance lead to the reasons why the distinction can be defined only after preliminary recognition that iterability is common to each of the entities distinguished.

> But this relative purity is not constructed *against* citationality or iterability, but against other kinds of iteration within a general iterability which is the effraction into the allededly rigorous purity of every event of discourse or every speech act. Thus, one must less oppose citation or iteration to the noniteration of an event, than construct a differential typology of forms of iteration. [326]

> Above all, I will not conclude from this that . . . there is no effect of the performative, no effect of ordinary language, no effect of presence and of speech acts. It is simply that these effects do not exclude what is generally opposed to them term by term, but on the contrary presuppose it in dissymmetrical fashion, as the general space of their possibility. [327]

Those passages are typical of how Derrida maneuvers around the relative specificity of speech acts throughout "Signature Event Context." Instead of defining what the specificity consists of, Derrida concentrates on what it cannot be.

This unidirectional conceptualization of speech acts is also prominent among theorists who have developed Derrida's points. Despite a broad consensus that something does indeed make performatives different, far more attention has been devoted to showing what that something is not than to defining what it is. In her essay "Mallarmé and Austin," for example, Barbara Johnson makes the point that the difference between dramatis personae and actual persons must not be allowed to obfuscate the conventionality of both. "The performative utterance thus automatically fictionalizes its utterer when it makes him the mouthpiece of a conventionalized authority. Where else, for example, but at a party *convention* could a presidential candidate be nominated?" (*Critical Difference*, 60) Whether I declare war as head of state or as an actor playing the role of head of state, the authority for my declaration is no more than a ritualized agreement. I speak with effect only because my listeners observe a certain set of formulas that determine what the effect will be.

Johnson's recognition of the performative's relative specificity is like Derrida's in that it asserts without defining. A capital trial and an imaginative fiction are "of course" not the same; nevertheless, previous definitions of what differentiates them have operated on false assumptions: "It is, of course, not our intention to nullify all differences between a poem and, say, a verdict, but only to problematize the assumptions on which such distinctions are based. If people are put to death by a verdict and not by a poem, it is not because the law is not a fiction" (60). Negatives predominate. Johnson's elegant argument against Austin follows Derrida's in simultaneously asserting the differences between versions of performative speech and concentrating on why those differences cannot be what they are commonly considered.

The committed reflections on Derrida and Austin in Stanley Fish's "With the Compliments of the Author" bring Fish's notion of interpretive community to bear on the vexed question of the performative's relative purity. When the pertinent members of a collectivity understand the conventions invoked by speech in the same way, the performance succeeds in becoming an act. "This, then, is how successful performatives occur, by means of the shared assumptions which enable speakers and hearers to make the same kind of sense of the words they exchange" (708). The contrast between fact and fiction—between a wedding in a chapel and a wedding on a stage—is therefore a contrast between the kinds of shared assumptions activated. A stage wedding does not effect a married couple because the conventions recognized by an interpretive community prohibit that kind of performance from having that particular effect.

Fish joins Derrida and Johnson in concentrating much more assiduously on the features common to all speech acts than on defining what allows some to maintain their relative purity. Deep though his concern is with "the obvious differences between fiction and real life" (709), mention of those differences ordinarily leads to discussion of what they are not.

The differences, whatever they are (and they are not always the same), do not arrange themselves around a basic or underlying difference between unmediated experience and experience that is the product of interpretive activity.... Again, this does not mean that there is no difference between them, only that they are all conventional as are the facts they entail.

The result is not to deny distinctions but to recharacterize them as distinctions between different kinds of interpretive practice. [709]

Derrida's insistence was on general iterability, Fish's on general interpretive practice. Both men introduce distinctions within the general schema primarily as a prelude to defense of the schema's generality.

Fish concludes "With the Compliments of the Author" with an extended argument that Derrida and Austin are actually much more compatible than the former believes. The argument's central focus—very much in agreement with this book's theses— is the rigor with which Austin ultimately collapses the performative/constative distinction that opens *How to Do Things with Words*. Like the rest of his article, however, Fish's conclusion follows the unidirectional track taken in the original Derridean essay that is its intertext. In analogy to the relative specificity of the actual (as opposed to the fictional) performative, the singularity of the constative is not an issue as Fish follows the delightful self-contradictions through which Austin shreds the system he is erecting. Fish joins Shoshana Felman in viewing Austin as a full deconstructionist joyously "writing a prose that complicates its initial assertions and obfuscates the oppositions on which it supposedly turns" (Fish, 717): "The one thing that remains constant in *How to Do Things with Words* is that nothing remains constant: no term, no definition, no distinction survives the length of the argument, and many do not survive the paragraph or sentence in which they are first presented" (716). I find this argument a thoroughly convincing description of one of Austin's most endearing traits. But it ignores the component of speech-act theory exemplified in the realist constative, humanity's collective ability to solidify terms, definitions, and distinctions despite their propensity for disintegration. If reading Austin is a continual revelation of words' delightful play among themselves, it is also an encounter with instance after instance of words' productive labor among their users. That labor is the principal object of the realist constative.

Derrida, Johnson, and Fish orient their analyses of Austin toward eliminating the line of demarcation between speech that does things and speech that repeats what was said without re-producing what was done. Their conclusions foreground the imitative, iterable, conventional, and playful character of every linguistic event, even one weighted with material consequences. Agreeing that there is no demarcation, however, also highlights the potential for active seriousness in linguistic events that seem far removed from responsibility for what they say; the duchesse de Langeais's "Goriot" metonymy is deadly as well as exuber-ant. That speech acts are speech means that their context cannot be exhaustively determined; that they are acts means that an indeterminate context can be reliably defined by what is said within it.

Barbara Johnson focuses on the irony inherent in the terms that Austin chose to define what was left after he decided to ignore imitation speech acts. The lexicon enlisted to say what is not imitation is a brace of words for imitation's most blatant form.

> For the very word [Austin] uses to name "mere doing," the very name he gives to that from which he excludes theatricality, is none other than the word that most commonly *names* theatri-cality: the word *perform*. As if this were not ironic enough, exactly the same split can be found in Austin's other favorite word: *act*. How is it that a word that expresses most simply the mere doing of an act necessarily leads us to the question of—acting? [65]

Johnson's Austin undermines his distinctions in the founding process of stating them for his readers. His desire to separate act from imitation produces a lexical summary of why no such separation is feasible.

But what happens if we reverse Johnson's strategy and start

with the theatrical rather than the factual sense of *perform* and *act*? What if we explore the ambiguity of acting not from the impossibility of its being "mere doing" but from its concomitant inability to be "mere copying"? Then the duality of *perform* and *act* means that there is no more a space safely protected from the real world than there is a space safely anchored within it. Precisely that duality explains why the exposition of *Le Père Goriot* contains the admonition about the necessity of the word *drama*: dramatic performances in no way preclude effects that are dramatic in another sense. Speech acts cannot be named without substituting personae for persons, but personae cannot be situated without the potential to function as persons.

Johnson concludes her discussion of Austin's terminology by asking how it is possible "to discuss the question of authenticity when that question already subverts the very terms we use to discuss it" (66). We can also ask how it is possible *not* to discuss the question of authenticity when its subversion of necessity introduces terms that put the question on the table. The constative reality of Austin's speaking agents is inauthentic only if we assume a nonconstative definition of authenticity.

Austin's decision not to address staged imitations of performatives was misguided and unjustifiable. But the assumption that theatricality makes iterability and conventionality all that we need to know neglects the fact that the most theatrical of events can also be the most consequential. During the French Revolution, the seriousness of the staged was apparent in the theaters themselves, where performing the role of an aristocrat or priest could lead to grave personal injury. Chateaubriand's remarks are typical of countless narratives describing the Revolution's attitude toward those who *perform* and *act* in reactionary ways. "In the theaters the actors announced news, the audience intoned patriotic couplets. Topical plays drew the crowds; a priest would appear on stage; people would shout "Hypocrite! Hypocrite!" and the priest would respond, "Gentlemen, *Vive la Nation!*" (I, 232) The republican slogan *Vive la Nation!* announced that what was being acted was only a performance. Its protective production is a clear demonstration that the question of seriousness and authenticity cannot be ignored just because a performance's context ought to identify it as fictitious. Like that of the efficacious performative, the specificity of a speech act's staged imitation is at best "relative." Among the principal revelations of the realist constative is the high seriousness of fictionalized performance.

The "Signature" section of Derrida's "Signature Event Context" deconstructs that classic attribute of individual identity, the name as personally written and objectively attested. Like any other performance, that of a signature is befuddled by the fact that the iterability permitting it to work also prevents it from working.

> The effects of signature are the most ordinary thing in the world. The condition of possibility for these effects is simultaneously, once again, the condition of their impossibility, of the impossibility of their rigorous purity. In order to function, that is, in order to be legible, a signature must have a repeatable, iterable, imitable form; it must be able to detach itself from the present and singular intention of its production. It is its sameness which, in altering its identity and singularity, divides the seal. [328–29]

From a statement that the effects are real, Derrida again proceeds backward to the effects' origin and shows why they cannot authorize what they claim. My response is again to reverse the reversal and assert that the condition of impossibility is simultaneously the condition of possibility. If the effects of signature are the most ordinary thing in the world, they do not disappear from the world simply because their cause is indiscernible, indefinable, and unlocalizable.

The argument against the Derridean critique of speech acts is the same as that against Barthes's concept of the impact of castration on realist discourse. Both critics assume that a consequence cannot survive abolition of its premises. In *Le Père Goriot* as in *Sarrasine*, however, textual dismemberment of causes goes hand in hand with textual perpetuation of effects.

Take the signature of the three characters Goriot, Vautrin, and Rastignac. The first has its origin in the reality of personal existence yet loses both its paternal dignity and its individual form. The second originates only in a decision to perform yet endures and imposes until society takes counteraction against the repudiation of its rules that "Vautrin" entails. The last, "Rastignac," is in fact the Name of the Father but is at the same time a constant display that what is in fact is inconsequential. The three names dominating *Le Père Goriot* are three demonstrations that origins can neither explain nor explain away effects.

After Mme de Beauséant's first performance of her kinship with him, Rastignac unknowingly acquires a new identity. "Because his aunt was a Marcillac, the poor student had been well received in this house without knowing the extent of the favor. To be admitted into these gilded rooms was equivalent to documentary proof of great nobility. By appearing in this society, the most exclusive of all, he had gained the right to go everywhere" (43). Nothing grounds the signature more authoritatively than documentary proof of nobility, and even that ground admits a fully authorized surrogate: "To be admitted into these gilded rooms was *equivalent* to documentary proof of great nobility." Simultaneously the origin is displaced beyond recovery, its effects invigorated beyond measure. The career built on Rastignac's recognition by a social group is the realist constative at its most dynamic.

Its dynamism, without objective origin, is the pure effect of conventional procedures. But its conventionality does not disable but empowers it, for social performance of a constative fact is sufficient for its factuality. By concentrating on the absence of overtly staged speech acts from *How to Do Things with Words*, deconstructionists have neglected Austin's sensitivity to the power of covert staging to produce the real. Deconstructionist arguments, directly pertinent to textual obliteration of "Goriot," are less helpful for defining textual animation of "Rastignac." Like Austin, Balzac delineates a universe in which the association between an iterable performance and an absence is simply not pertinent to the performance's institution of a presence.

4

Louis XVII and the Chevalier
de la Vernaye:
The Red, the Black, the Restoration

No incident in Stendhal's *Le Rouge et le noir* has elicited more commentary than Julien's attempt to murder Mme de Rênal. The ostensible explanation—that Mme de Rênal's letter to the marquis de la Mole has irrevocably prevented Julien's marriage to Mathilde—just does not hold up. Mathilde is pregnant, and she refuses to consider an abortion. As a consequence, her father's vow never to permit her marriage is pure bluster. The marriage will certainly take place if Julien simply waits out the storm while his child's gestation continues. The end of Julien's career is in fact not Mme de Rênal's letter of denunciation but his own bloody reaction to it. A protagonist remarkable for his self-possession suddenly seems to become intent on self-destruction, a radical psychological shift that has been the subject of extensive critical speculation from the novel's original appearance to our time.

Less discussed but no less implausible than the attempted murder is its consequence, Julien's conviction, death sentence, and execution. If everything we know about Julien's character makes his crime a puzzle, everything we know about his society makes his punishment an impossibility. At the age of fourteen, Julien decided to become a priest because he saw a scrupulously honest judge deliver one shameful verdict after another in order not to incur the Church's displeasure. From that incident on, the legal system depicted in *Le Rouge et le noir* has been the tool of influential individuals rather than the agent of justice—after all, "where is the judge without a son or at least a cousin to place in society?" (217; all translations from Stendhal are my own)—and the novel's most influential characters all passionately desire Julien's acquittal. The epigraph to the chapter that describes their machinations strongly hints that they will succeed: it narrates the liberation through bribery of a Frenchman who not only killed his sister but was guilty of another murder as well. Julien's crime, far less heinous than sororicide, should be correspondingly easier to dismiss.

When M. de Rênal, tormented by the anonymous revelation of his cuckoldry, contemplated killing his wife, he had no fear of being punished for the murder: "Whatever happens, our congregation and my friends on the jury will save me" (146). In contrast to M. de Rênal, Julien is guilty only of attempted murder. Furthermore, his friends are much more imposing than M. de Rênal's. Vigorously defending him are Mathilde de la Mole, Mme de Rênal, the all-powerful abbé de Frilair, the maréchale de Fervaques, and monseigneur l'évêque de ***, "through whom one becomes a bishop in France ... this prelate who controlled the Church of France and made bishops" (462, 472). Yet all their efforts are futile. Julien dies on the guillotine.

Gérard Genette writes of the "contemptuous silence" with which Stendhal envelops the psychological reversal necessary for his protagonist to shoot Mme de Rênal (77). No less contemptuous is Stendhal's explanation of the social reversal necessary for a legal proceeding to conclude contrary to the wishes of Restoration notables. According to the novel's tortured motivation of its conclusion, Julien is found guilty because the abbé de Frilair makes a grievous strategic error. Instead of straightforwardly instructing the jurors he controls to vote for acquittal, he tells them to vote like their foreman, Valenod. Valenod then disobeys Frilair's explicit instructions to him in a rebellion made possible because he has already been named to the prefecture that Frilair planned to give him after the trial ended in the agreed way. Even if we ignore the implausibility of Frilair's scrupling to fix a jury in overt terms, this scenario remains outrageous.

Valenod, who has just seen M. de Rênal lose the office of mayor of Verrières, knows perfectly well that Restoration officials are unmade the same way they are made. Like a mayor, a prefect has to please Church and nobility after winning office as well as while seeking it. Frilair sees acquittal as leading "to the realization of all my desires" (462), and he is not the man to forgive treachery in so important an enterprise. Valenod's tenure as prefect will undoubtedly be the shortest on record, and it is certain that he knows it. The powers that rule France and its courts are massed to assure Julien's release, and the text's effort to explain his conviction makes no concessions to credibility.

The fascinating point about this attempt to explain the inexplicable is that only in a society as vile as Restoration France would any explanation be required. What happens is actually nothing more that what is supposed to happen in a state under the rule of law: a criminal receives the punishment prescribed by statute for those guilty of his crime. The judicial procedures represented in *Le Rouge et le noir*, however, are such that it is only because of a double-cross that society treats attempted murder as attempted murder. A convoluted series of corruptions terminates as if no corruption had taken place. Furthermore, the text attributes even this accidental implementation of the legal code to actions dissociated from the modes of social coexistence described in the rest of the novel. The conclusion of *Le Rouge et le noir* is remarkable for its uncomfortable effort to motivate a radical departure from the social thematics informing what precedes it. Previously, the meaning of events was the product of a collective decision by the leaders of Church and aristocracy. At Julien's trial, the leaders of Church and aristocracy collectively decide that the defendant is blameless, but their power seems to have vanished. Suddenly, events and their consequences, a crime and its punishment, succeed one another regardless of the interpretations placed on them by characters whose hermeneutic authority is otherwise incontrovertible. Earlier, guilt and innocence were determined not by what someone did but by what socially powerful individuals said. At Julien's trial, many powerful individuals say he is innocent, but what he did remains determinant. In a staggering departure from textual precedent, *Le Rouge et le noir* ends on a character being found guilty of a crime he actually committed.

In addition to guilt and innocence, social rank acquires textually unprecedented solidity at the conclusion of *Le Rouge et le noir*. In his speech to his jury, Julien describes himself as if his peasant birth definitively established a class identity he could never hope to alter.

> Gentlemen, I do not have the honor of belonging to your class, you see in me a peasant who rebelled against his inferior situation. . . . I see men who will elect to punish in me and so discourage forever that class of young men who, born into a lower class and in some way oppressed by poverty, are fortunate enough to obtain a good education and daring enough to mix with what the pride of the rich calls society.
>
> That is my crime, gentlemen, and it will be punished with all the more severity because, as things are, I am not being judged by my peers. I do not see among the jurors any peasant who has enriched himself, I see only indignant bourgeois. [476]

The abbé de Frilair defines this speech as a declaration of class war so inflammatory that Julien's death is a kind of suicide. In Frilair's understanding, the defendant's words stimulated a "caste interest" (488) in his jurors, who voted for death in order to eliminate a grave threat to their social position.

Frilair, however, attributes to Julien's bourgeois jurors an extraordinarily disinterested devotion to the interests of the aristocracy. The contradiction is implicit in Frilair's use of "caste" to replace Julien's "class." Class is the effect of financial situation, caste the effect of birth. The latter was the basis for the Restoration's attempt to reproduce the aristocratic social organization of the ancien régime, the former the concept the bourgeoisie put forth to oppose both the ancien régime and its reproduction. Every aristocracy posits a divinely guaranteed harmony between an individual's social status and social function. God in His omniscience decides which person is suited for which task and reveals His decision through conception; from kings to beggars, every member of society *naturally* occupies the position most favorable to the divine plan. Caste implements the social organization which God Himself intends humanity to observe.

Caste consequently condemns the bourgeoisie to eternally subaltern functions, and the jurors come from the bourgeoisie. Their "caste interest" is at loggerheads with their class interest. Although Julien's speech does indeed subvert the caste principles of Restoration aristocracy, his listeners are not the beneficiaries but the victims of those principles. It is not nobles who sit in judgment but, as Julien said, "only bourgeois," only members of the Third Estate whose interests are thwarted by social equation of birth with worth. The subtitle of *Le Rouge et le noir* is *Chronique de 1830*, chronicle of the year when the French bourgeoisie's resentment against the ideology of birth produced a revolution for the sake of exactly the kind of class mobility Julien claims as a right. The abbé de Frilair's argument that twelve bourgeois jurors understood that claim as a threat to their most vital interests presumes a political docility about to be violently repudiated by the rest of France's middle class. Although Julien does in fact sound like Figaro, his audience consists of Jourdains rather than Almavivas, and bourgeois gentlemen do not normally see a capital offense in the contention that a man can rise above the position to which he was born.

Julien's demand that oppressed young men be allowed to ascend the social scale is strikingly similar to the bourgeois ideology that prepared the Revolution of 1789 as well as to the bourgeois frustration that produced the Revolution of 1830. If one wanted a brief summary of the speech with which Julien supposedly threatened the bourgeoisie with political doom, it would be hard to improve on the question with which Sieyès opened *Qu'est-ce que le tiers état?*, his famous pamphlet in favor of the bourgeoisie's political exaltation: "What are they asking for? To become SOMETHING." Besides asking its readers to believe that irresistible political influence is powerless to save Julien from the guillotine, the conclusion of *Le Rouge et le noir* defines archetypically bourgeois sentiments as anathema to archetypically bourgeois characters. Julien's fatal speech should not affront but stroke his listeners' "caste interest."

The career of the jury's foreman, Valenod, has mounted an

attack on caste at least as vigorous as Julien's. Like the defendant, the chief juror began life as one of "that class of young
men ... born into a lower class and in some way oppressed by
poverty." And, like the defendant, the chief juror endured the
resentment of his fellows after he rose above the place assigned
him by birth. Although Valenod and M. de Rênal exploit Verrières together, the aristocratic mayor benefits from an indulgence denied his plebeian accomplice. "People were jealous of
the mayor, the liberals had grounds for complaint; but after all
he was noble and made for a superior position, whereas M.
Valenod's father had not left him six hundred livres of income.
People who had taken pity on the apple green suit everyone saw
him wearing in his youth had been forced to come to envy his
Norman horses, his gold chains, his clothes straight from Paris,
all his current prosperity" (162). Since Valenod is no more
"noble and made for a superior position" than Julien, it is hardly
credible that he and his jurors would interpret a classically bourgeois defense of upward mobility as a seditious act so threatening to the bourgeoisie that its perpetrator must be put to death.
Julien's speech is nothing more than a development of the
bourgeoisie's preferred rallying cry, *careers open to talents.*

Even Frilair's strictures about Julien's speech are irreconcilable with his own biography. Like Valenod, Frilair is a perfect
illustration of the upward mobility he supposedly finds intolerably threatening. "Twelve years earlier, M. l'abbé de Frilair
had come to Besançon with the tiniest of trunks which, according to reports, contained all he possessed. Now he was one
of the department's richest property owners" (217). The men
who are represented by the text as provoked to frenzy by Julien's
speech have in fact lived out each of the principles the speech
defends. What they experience as a personal affront could more
logically be understood as a statement of personal solidarity.

In yet another apparent concession to the class sensitivities
of his jurors, Julien addresses them as Julien Sorel, peasant son
of a Jura carpenter, whereas he has every right to speak as M.
le chevalier de la Vernaye, lieutenant in the fifteenth hussars
regiment, "one of the most brilliant in the army" (444). Although this new name comes from the marquis de la Mole's

determination that his daughter not marry a commoner, its validity is unimpeachable. Strong documentary evidence attests not only to Lieutenant de la Vernaye's identity but to his outstanding previous service as second lieutenant.

Julien Sorel begins to address his bourgeois jury with this sentence: "Gentlemen, I do not have the honor of belonging to your class." Lieutenant de la Vernaye has full authority to reverse the terms: "Gentlemen, you do not have the honor of belonging to my class." That it is the peasant Sorel rather than the knighted la Vernaye who takes the floor is among the least understandable components of a denouement consistently indifferent to comprehensibility. Even more than Julien's crime, his trial and execution stand apart from the preceding portion of the novel. If we take the final chapters' lack of titles and epigraphs as a formal correlative to the substantive disparities that distinguish them from the seventy-four chapters that come before, each with its own title and epigraph, then the point of dissociation is precisely the trial and verdict.

Julien's speech and death sentence thus constitute a stark line of demarcation within *Le Rouge et le noir*. On one side of the line, Restoration ideology is a fictitious construct; on the other, it appears to describe real social practices with real collective adherence. Judicial procedures that were unconnected to facts now culminate in the outcome prescribed by law; bourgeois characters who were contemptuous of the idea that "noble" and "made for a superior position" were synonymous expressions now react with horror to an attack on that synonymy; men who have themselves *become* rich and powerful abruptly believe that riches and power should belong only to those *born* with them; a character who despised his peasant family and all it stood for now vindicates his peasant condition with passionate pride. In the aberrant conclusion to *Le Rouge et le noir*, a crime is a crime regardless of who exonerates the criminal, a peasant is a peasant despite documentary proof of his nobility, and the philosophy of caste describes an immutable fact of life accepted by those it would oppress as well as those it glorifies. In each instance, social discourse accurately represents reality and appears thoroughly referential. The Austinian constative is irrelevant to a world where social identity is not a conventional creation but an objective given, and it is in just such a world that Julien Sorel is condemned to death. Words that did things have lost their ability to perform, and the things words say have become passive descriptions of the way things are.

But the anomalous character of the referential discourse concluding *Le Rouge et le noir* foregrounds the constative discourse preceding it. The text insistently dissociates the collective processes making Julien a criminal from those making him the chevalier de la Vernaye, a radical ideological break that highlights what precedes as well as what follows. In one of the novel's crucial chapters (II, 8), Mathilde de la Mole observes the most brilliant representatives of her age at the ball in the hôtel de Retz. The titles, honors, and decorations she sees strike her as so many shams; none signifies anything except itself, none actually represents reality, each is glaringly performative. The only "decoration" that is the consequence of its bearer's behavior is the death sentence pronounced on Count Altamira in his South American homeland. Only here is a word attached to a thing, only here does language designate something outside itself. " 'The only thing I see distinguishing a man is a death sentence,' thought Mathilde... 'a title of baron, of vicomte, is bought; a cross is given; my brother just got one, what did he do? A rank is obtained' " (296). Three passive verbs—*is bought, is given, is obtained*—embody the passive nature of the Restoration's distinguishing marks. All decorations are assumed to be referential because they theoretically recognize merit previously displayed, all are actually constative because they express nothing beyond the force that accompanies and succeeds their utterance.

The chapter narrating Mathilde's insight is entitled "Which Decoration Distinguishes?" In semiotic terminology, that question would read "Which sign refers?" For an Austinian formulation, take "Which name is not a performance?" All the titles that, according to Restoration ideology, designate the divinely guaranteed nature of the world in fact do nothing more than activate a conventional agreement. Only a death sentence reliably denotes an action. The death sentence concluding *Le Rouge et le noir* appears in a text that has already defined the sentence as unique among signs for indicating rather than creating facts.

But the final death sentence is not unique in its immediate context, where the signs of social rank have the same substance as the classification of criminal behavior. Lieutenant de la Vernaye ("a rank is obtained") represents himself as a peasant, and his jurors confirm that no other representation would be acceptable. The objective fact of birth authoritatively establishes the linguistic form of identity. Earlier, the existence of the chevalier de la Vernaye compellingly illustrated Mathilde's thesis that only a death sentence has referential validity in her society. At Julien's trial, the chevalier vanishes, and birth acquires the same determinant impact as death.

Before the trial, referential language is so alien to Restoration discourse that the word "fact" is indistinguishable from the word "fiction." Facts remain factual regardless of who believes them, fictions depend on their reader's connivance. Just such connivance is the sine qua non of what Stendhal's Restoration accepts as a fact. For example, the norms of aristocratic society restrict dueling to social peers. When Julien's duel with the chevalier de Beauvoisis violates those norms, the violation is eliminated by instantaneous verbal creation of equality in rank. "That very evening, the chevalier de Beauvoisis and his friend repeated everywhere that this M. Sorel, who was by the way a perfect young man, was the natural son of one of the marquis de la Mole's intimate friends. This fact passed without difficulty" (282). The ease with which this *fact* passed prefigures that establishing the chevalier de la Vernaye's nobility and military experience. After "public opinion declared in his favor" (444), M. de la Vernaye's status is secure. He ceases to be the peasant Julien Sorel with precisely the same smoothness manifest when the peasant Julien Sorel later ceases to the the chevalier de la Vernaye. Because words do not describe the world but only stimulate a conventional interpretation, designation of a fact requires nothing more than manipulation of public opinion.

The interaction of social identity and performative semantics in *Le Rouge et le noir* perhaps receives its clearest formulation soon after Julien takes up his secretarial duties in Paris. When the marquis de la Mole, confined to his room by gout, wants to treat his secretary as an equal, he gives him a blue suit. Dressed in black, Julien is a secretary; dressed in blue, he is the son of a duke. "My dear Sorel, allow me to make you the gift of a blue suit; when it pleases you to wear it and to come to my rooms, you will be, in my eyes, the younger brother of the comte de Chaulnes, which is to say the son of my friend the old duke" (283–84). This stratagem preserves the form of orthodox social relations by assuring that a tone of equality is adopted solely between individuals holding the same rank. At the same time, it turns the standard view of the basis for social relations on its head. It is not rank that authorizes a tone of equality but a tone of equality that establishes rank. Signs do not reflect but originate the condition they articulate. In spectacular fashion, Julien's blue suit epitomizes the production of concrete referents from arbitrary signs characteristic of social interaction in *Le Rouge et le noir*.

Austin's originative condition for a felicitous performative is a conventional procedure having conventional effect. The marquis de la Mole's instructions institute the conventional procedure as a visit in a blue suit and specify the conventional effect in unequivocal terms: "You will be, in my eyes, the younger brother of the comte de Chaulnes." As legitimate son of the duc de Chaulnes, as illegitimate son of another friend of the marquis de la Mole, and as the chevalier de la Vernaye, Julien manifests the central social theme in *Le Rouge et le noir*: identity identifies nothing except the conventions observed by those who recognize it. Stendhal's Restoration is a performative universe.

Le Rouge et le noir incorporates a graduated series of links between the blatant artificiality of the identity conferred by Julien's suit and the concealed artificiality of identities conferred by other social conventions. On Julien's return from England, the marquis de la Mole presents him with a cross and redefines the procedures that will bring forth an aristocrat from a secretary. "I no longer want to have you abandon your black suit, and I'm accustomed to the more amusing tone I've taken with the man wearing the blue suit. Until further notice, this is understood: when I see this cross, you will be the younger son of my friend the duc de Chaulnes." (288). The status conferred by a blue suit depended on a convention observed by only two men. That conferred by the cross is ratified by the whole of French society. In a clear echo of Mathilde's insight into the performative force of all decorations, her father uses the cross to change the world by changing a name. As Julien notes with intense satisfaction, the change is extensive. Every facet of his interaction with the marquis varies according to the signifiers he puts on.

This move from blue cloth to a coveted decoration also goes from a semiprivate agreement to a universally observed convention. The development continues until it absorbs every form of identification in *Le Rouge et le noir*. Who is the marquis de la Mole? A man other people treat as if they had said to him what he says to Julien, "You will be, in my eyes, the marquis de la Mole." In *Le Rouge et le noir*, the marquis's noble birth inherently confers nothing more substantial than Julien's blue suit. Both marks of identity are significant only because society agrees on what they signify. During the revolutionary decades before the Restoration—the decades that Stendhal's notables devote their lives to repressing—France proved in blood and fire that what nobility means is not a natural fact but a social custom. When customs changed, nobility became a capital crime instead of a cardinal virtue. To be born a marquis and to wear a blue suit are identical insofar as each accords status only because someone else recognizes the status it accords. Whether aristocratic blood or a new color of clothes, any mark of social position is an empty signifier. The signified attached to it is historically not eternally determined.

The impossibility of distinguishing between the status attached to aristocratic parents and that attached to a different suit is implicit in the bloodline that Julien acquires by wearing blue. In the marquis's words, Julien becomes the son of the duc de Chaulnes, who is also the father of the marquise de la Mole (250). The marquis therefore not only ennobles Julien but makes him his own brother-in-law and the uncle of Mathilde and Norbert. A blue suit puts Julien into both of the families whose "natural" superiority the marquis de la Mole should have the greatest interest in preserving. Instead, the marquis recapitulates the text in which he appears by equating the natural with the conventional, a suit of clothes with blood and marriage, at the base of social order. The duc de Chaulnes, "well known for his aristocratic prejudices" (250), is the archetypal proponent of a referential understanding of social titles. The text's predilection for collapsing referents into conventions is apparent in the duc de Chaulnes's central role in a stunning display that titles are the opposite of what he wants to believe.

The play with conventional alteration of Julien's paternity in *Le Rouge et le noir* reminds contemporary readers of Jacques Lacan. For Lacan, the immense symbolic function attached to the Name of the Father depends on the Name's dissociation from procreative reality; the capacity "to observe the real is precisely that which has not the slightest importance in the matter" of paternity's social definition (*Ecrits*, 199). Because it institutes humanity's symbolic articulation of its universe, the Name of the Father is essential even in tribes that do not understand the male contribution to reproduction, and "it is certainly this that demonstrates that the attribution of procreation to the father can only be the effect of a pure signifier" (199). To meet the needs of a pure signifier, a blue suit serves as well as patrilineal descent.

But in realist fiction, the signifier can fulfill its social responsibility only if its purity is concealed and it is assumed to convey not an arbitrary but an inalienable signified. The marquis de la Mole cannot change the way he treats Julien without mediating the change through a new identity; the Name requires the Father, the blue suit the duc de Chaulnes. The constative semantics of *Le Rouge et le noir* achieves conventional effect only when conventional procedures define signs as referential. Dressed in black, Julien expresses the same emptiness as when he is dressed in blue. The clothes of an aspirant to the priesthood alter his "perfect unbelief" (284) no more than the clothes of an aristocratic dandy alter his peasant birth. Nevertheless, his heavenly father furnishes a signified at least as substantial as the duc de Chaulnes. The protagonist of *Le Rouge et le noir* continuously demonstrates that the two fundamental institutions of the Restoration, the Church and the aristocracy, are erected on emptiness yet convey absolute plenitude. The characters of *Le Rouge et le noir* continuously do for themselves exactly what the regime of Louis XVIII and Charles X did for itself, convert quintessentially performative operations into incontrovertibly referential truths.

The Restoration's restoration of the connection between the Name and the Father, the signifier and the referent, was its most urgent historical task. Because the French Revolution had exposed the signs of Church, monarchy, and aristocracy as formal exercises in vacuous expression, the pure signifier lost its capacity to structure social existence. As a result, the reconstituted Bourbon regime sought to obliterate France's memory of the void behind language in order to reestablish signs' perfect referential validity. The marquis de la Mole could not treat Julien as an equal without previously making him the son of a duke; other members of France's dominant class could not feel confident of identity without previously assuming that the names articulating social status were infallible expressions of reality. If the names and reality were in contradiction, it was reality that had to adapt.

I take the literary play with signs and referents in *Le Rouge et le noir* to be a faithful analogue to the historical work with signs and referents characteristic of the Restoration. Both the novel and the age furnish a sustained, monumental display of verbal creativity successfully masquerading as verbal reference. The Restoration's first sovereign, Louis XVIII, took his name through a process indistinguishable from that which made Julien Sorel the son of the duc de Chaulnes. From Louis I in the fourteenth century to Louis XVI in the eighteenth, France's monarchs assumed their regal numerals on assuming their throne. Kingly titles were the outward sign of an actual fact, a name granted on the occasion of an event. The son of Louis XVI never assumed the throne and consequently never became Louis XVII; two years after his father was guillotined, he died as a citizen rather than a monarch. "Louis XVII" is the signifier in all its purity, unpolluted by attachment to anything except other signifiers.

Yet the Restoration began by converting that pure signifier into the name of a person who ruled. Immediately after his nephew's death, the brother of Louis XVI took the title of Louis XVIII in retroactive affirmation that the semiotic sequence of French monarchs faithfully represented an immutable historical succession. Like Julien's entry into the duc de Chaulnes's family, the referential value of "Louis XVII" at first rested only on a semiprivate agreement, that accepted by the dwindling number of aristocratic émigrés who remained with the exiled French court during its hapless treks across Europe. Like the empty decorations that Mathilde observed at the hôtel de Retz, however, the royal stature of a pitiful child became an objective truth when the Bourbons regained the throne in 1814. As was the case with "chevalier de la Vernaye," all that was required for "Louis XVII" to generate a referent was the acquiescence of public opinion. A dead child became the king of France through institution of a conventional procedure with the predominant conventional effect of annihilating objective reality in order to invigorate social beliefs.

Le Rouge et le noir accomplishes its most direct historical reference through multifarious demonstrations that reference is always a historical fabrication. Julien's black suit, blue suit, and shifting fathers are so many chronicles of an age in which signs produce something from nothing because their interpreters' lives depend on it. The performative onomastics of *Le Rouge et le noir* represents the performative history of the Restoration, a regime that made its founding document—the Charter of 1814—into a storehouse of precedents for the exuberant creativity of the signs identifying Julien. In fact an indispensable reaction to the French people's resistance to full reinstitution of the Old Regime, the Charter of 1814 nevertheless defined itself as the free, unconstrained gift of Louis XVIII to his people. In the charter's preamble, the king presents what he is writing as a simple continuation of his predecessors' immemorial commitment to the liberty of their subjects. The charter names the kings whose work it prolongs as Louis le Gros, Saint Louis, Philippe le Bel, Louis XI, Henri II, Charles IX, and Louis XIV, a list obliterating not only the Revolution but most other discontinuities in French history as well. From the twelfth through the nineteenth centuries, France's kings are an integral whole; the charter responds not to the Declaration of the Rights of Man but uniquely to "the example of the kings our predecessors" and "the venerable monuments of ages past." "By uniting older times and modern times," "by thus seeking to reconnect the chain of the ages," the charter made unbroken repetition the program of a nation.

The charter's most stupefying use of language to change history is its final words: "Given in Paris, in the year of grace 1814 and the eighteenth year of our reign." While "given" factualizes the fiction of Louis's power *not* to give what his subjects demand, dating the charter in the nineteenth year of his reign makes the difference between fact and fiction officially indeterminable. The first eighteen years of Louis XVIII's reign, like all the years of Louis XVII's, exist solely in the words naming them. They entered history on entering language and in the process severed political truth from historical reality. The clause with which *Le Rouge et le noir* narrates Julien's first acquisition of an aristocratic identity is perfectly applicable to the Restoration's acquisition of political power; "this fact passed," and the definition of a "fact" became whatever a community chose to make it. What was historically eighteen years of powerless exile became linguistically eighteen years of absolute power.

How do human beings survive under a monarch who uses language to destroy facts? By taking care never to use language to express those facts. To return to Lacan, Restoration discourse was an arduous effort to conceal the absence of the Father by venerating the presence of the Name, and the safest way to prevent denotational slips was to make sure that language remained endlessly repetitive. Since the goal of the Restoration was to convince itself that the world its words established was actually there, reference to a different world was rigorously prohibited. Instead of referring to what was, conversation could only repeat what was heard; language was socially acceptable in direct proportion to its alienation from social reality. The boredom Auerbach brilliantly situates at the core of *Le Rouge et le noir* is the effect of a speech community's determination to use language in such a way that it can never say anything. "The slightest living idea seemed obscene. Despite the correct tone, the perfect decorum, the desire to please, boredom was visible on every face. The young men who came to pay their respects, afraid of mentioning something that might suggest a thought or reveal some forbidden reading, fell silent after a few truly elegant comments on Rossini and the day's weather" (*Le Rouge et le noir*, 265). Stendhal's epigraph to the chapter entitled "Ways of Acting in 1830" is "Speech was given to man to conceal his thought." The route to success in 1830 is mapped by the epigraph to another chapter (II, 28): "He got by through calling what was white black and what was black white." And through calling the Directorate and Empire the first eighteen years of Louis XVIII's reign.

The criterion of linguistic propriety in *Le Rouge et le noir* is total hostility to linguistic reference. "Afraid of mentioning something that might suggest a thought," Stendhal's characters are condemned to say only what they know has already been said. An unprecedented choice and arrangement of words evokes the unthinkable possibility that social organization might diverge from precedent as well; expressing a thought not universally shared introduces the revolutionary concept that people do not unanimously agree that Louis XVII ruled France. Since the Restoration depended for its survival on the belief that what always had been was still and would always be, the conversations it authorized were interminable reiteration of the already said.

Before the French Revolution, the word *revolution* assured return of the old; afterward, it proclaimed creation of the new. The Restoration directed its campaign against the Revolution toward eradicating just this sort of change in sense, and the only way to immobilize sense is to assure that the signs expressing it remain inert. The effect was the stultifying dinners in the hôtel de la Mole, with conversation restricted to an exchange of words chosen because their exchange has already been certified harmless. "Ready-made sentences suited the mind of the lady of the house quite well" (260), and her guests share her predilection. The dominant class's compulsion to expunge innovation from existence acquires the textual form of a shared revulsion at innovation in speech.

Henri Lefebvre has characterized our own time as the age of a general eclipse of "referentials"; the words we most respect appear not to refer to the world but only to reproduce themselves. Long before Lefebvre, Stendhal defined the Restoration through an analogous gulf between speech and reference. Although love and death must figure among the ultimate human referentials, Stendhal's Restoration transforms both into rote ceremonies enacted apart from existential involvement. "In Paris love is the son of novels" (66), its expression a frozen discourse changing every twenty years "according to the currently fashionable pastime" (316). Death scripts are equally constrictive. For Mathilde, "the duel is now nothing but a ceremony. Everything about it is known beforehand, even what you're to say as you fall" (333). Death in social upheaval leaves no more room for improvisation than death during social rites. "Well then! Say the Revolution started up again. What roles would Croisenois and my brother play? It's written beforehand. Sublime resignation" (320). If one wanted to summarize socially acceptable behavior in *Le Rouge et le noir*, it would be hard to improve on Mathilde's variant phrasing of a single idea: "Everything about it is known beforehand... it's written beforehand." Decency demands immobility; in a society committed to the belief that history must be repetitive, life and death become applications of a precedent. *Imprévu* is a dirty word throughout *Le Rouge et le noir* because whatever is not written in advance threatens apocalypse.

The Charter of 1814 took pains to express Louis XVIII's solidarity with "the example of the kings our predecessors... the venerable monuments of ages past." Under the regime founded by the charter, the past's monuments circumscribe individual experience as tightly as political institutions. So thorough is social prohibition of everything except repetition that even Mathilde's will to flout prohibitions leads to a different form of repetition. She first understands her attraction to Julien through *Manon Lescaut*, *La Nouvelle Héloise*, and *Lettres d'une religieuse portugaise* (317), then comes to love through Boniface de la Mole and Marguerite de Navarre. Like Louis XVIII invoking the memory of Louis le Gros and Louis le Grand, Mathilde defines her life through her affinity with the dead. The origin of the Restoration was a monarch's assertion that he was repeating the past, that of Mathilde's love her desire to follow his example.

In his priestly black suit, the atheist Julien Sorel is a living exemplification of the barrier between signs and reference in *Le Rouge et le noir*. The career the atheist follows exemplifies one of the barrier's corollaries: because signs that do not denote can only repeat, expert repetition is the surest means of social advancement. Julien's meteoric ascent is due to his unique talent for making the already written work for him.

The two key decisions in Julien's life are to study for the priesthood and to make Mathilde definitively his. The former takes him to the Rênal household and then out of Verrières, the latter makes him the chevalier de la Vernaye and opens the way to wealth and power. Each decision is a farcical commentary on Restoration repetition: Julien's career begins in memorization and culminates in copying. His vertical move from the depths to the summit of society occurs because of a horizontal move from one set of dead words to another, from the New Testament and *Du pape* to letters written by a Russian to a woman Julien has never seen. The narrative armature of *Le Rouge et le noir* is a serial display of its protagonist's ability to use language so that it refers neither to external reality nor to internal sensations. Horatio Alger of the Restoration, Julien goes from rags to riches by recognizing that society listens most intently to what was said in another time and at another place.

Julien's first script is of course Scripture itself. "To win over the old priest Chélan, on whom he saw his future to depend, he had memorized the entire New Testament in Latin, he also knew the book *Du pape* by M. de Maistre and believed in one as little as the other" (49). By definition, memorized language is unrelated to the situation in which it is repeated and to the inner state of its speaker. Julien's conviction that the New Testament was nonreferential even at the time of its composition makes its estrangement from reality absolute. The words that do things in the Restoration are those which have no potential for saying things. Only static language produces a dynamic career.

Repetition of the New Testament begins to work miracles for Julien at the Rênal household and continues to do so at Valenod's. In the second theater, the audience's ecstasy increases with its inability to understand anything being said: " 'When will these fools get tired of hearing this biblical style they don't understand at all?' he thought. But on the contrary this style amused them with its strangeness, they laughed at it" (161). The full measure of glory attaches to mastery of language that has shed its pragmatic potential; in a world where reference could be fatal, free-floating signifiers offer the exhilaration of continued life; "they laughed at it." Repetition, recitation, Restoration—a major historical concern of *Le Rouge et le noir* is with collective euphoria in response to all discourse in which reference is unutterable.

Julien begins his rise by memorizing not only the New Testament but also Joseph de Maistre's *Du pape*, one of the crucial ideological documents of the Restoration. Commenting on Latin in the liturgy, *Du pape* makes explicit and grave what *Le Rouge et le noir* leaves implicit and comic, the vital importance of protecting language from human manipulation if rulers are to survive. "As for the people properly so called, if they do not understand the words, so much the better. Respect is enhanced, and the mind loses nothing. He who does not understand understands better than he who understands poorly.... From every imaginable point of view, religious language should be placed beyond the domain of men" (131; translations from Maistre are my own). With language "beyond the domain of men," human dominion over meaning vanishes as well. The rapt adoration elicited by Julien's content-free recitations is the effect of a society's unconscious sensation that representational language is its mortal enemy.

The man Julien calls "my M. de Maistre" (265) understood quite well that antirepresentational language is indistinguishable from absolute truth if no one challenges it. In *Le Rouge et le noir*, social identity is not referential but constative; in *Du pape*, papal infallibility is not descriptive but prescriptive. "It is in fact absolutely the same thing, in practice, not to be subject to error and not to be subject to accusations of error" (119). That the first eighteen years of Louis XVIII's reign were nonexistent matters not at all "in practice" if his subjects confirm their participation in his reign's nineteenth year. For the Restoration as seen by both Maistre and Stendhal, the referents that matter are not those which underlie language but those which follow it. The constative function addresses not what was but what will be.

The second set of holy writings responsible for Julien's triumphs consists of the fifty-three numbered letters transcribed so as to win Mathilde de la Mole by wooing Mme de Fervaques. Recall how those letters enter the text. Julien, in abject despair because of Mathilde's latest rejection, confides in the Russian prince Korasoff, whose advice is that Julien pretend to love someone else. When Julien replies that he lacks the will and the wit to sustain the necessary correspondence, Korasoff supplies him with a full set of letters written by another Russian during a seduction attempt in England some time earlier. For my purposes, the interesting point about this provenance is that it resonates with the Restoration's historical mission no less than the Bible and Maistre's *Du pape*. Written by one Russian and given to Julien by another, Korasoff's letters also connect the nineteenth century to the eighteenth as if the Revolution had never taken place: "Russians copy French behavior, but always fifty years late. They are now in the century of Louis XV" (*Le Rouge et le noir*, 394), which is to say the age Louis XVIII attempted to resuscitate.

Julien's use of this Russian correspondence almost seems to be designed as a textbook illustration of how language can communicate without the slightest pretense of referring. According to the celebrated schema in Jakobson's "Linguistics and Poetics," the six factors in an act of verbal communication are the addresser, the addressee, the context to which they refer, the contact between them, the code they use, and the message they send. The first three factors—addresser, addressee, and referential context—constitute the connections between language and the extralinguistic world, and those are precisely the factors eliminated during Julien's correspondence. As addresser, Julien does not exist. Transcribing automatically and unconsciously, he is a passive means for words to move from one sheet of paper to another. The first letter literally puts him to sleep, the rest figuratively do the same. "What he copied struck him as so absurd that he ended up transcribing line by line without thinking of meaning" (408). As addressee, Julien is even less present than as addresser. Even though he does so without thinking, he does at least write and, albeit unconsciously, legitimately functions as addresser. He does not read at all, however, and the addressee function is completely absent from his communication with Mme de Fervaques. Without even opening them, he throws the letters addressed to him into a drawer and continues to send his letters in numerical order as if no response had intervened.

When the addresser is unconscious and the addressee uninterested, the referential context is nonexistent. One of the letters Julien copies alludes to London and Richmond. "Without thinking of meaning," he reproduces the allusion without realizing that he should substitute "Paris" and "Saint-Cloud." The astonishing aspect of this farcical gaffe is not that Julien so easily explains it away when Mme de Fervaques confronts him but that it is apparently the only reference to reality in the whole, immensely long correspondence. Page after page, letter after letter written in England by a Russian to a Quaker serve without alteration to express Julien's devotion to a Catholic in Paris.

The starkly antireferential character of Julien's successful wooing has special importance because of the wooing's place in the novel. The most crucial single moment in Julien's ascendent career is his decision to employ Korasoff's letters according to the accompanying instructions. It is uniquely because of the letters that Julien conquers Mathilde and uniquely because of the conquest that he becomes the chevalier de la Vernaye. The paradox is that this critical juncture in the classic realist plot, the Parisian success of a young man from the provinces, is also the point of greatest disjuncture between language and its classic realist function, representation of a reality prior to and independent of its writing. As the novel reiterates with Rabelaisian verve, the sender of Julien's letters to Mme de Fervaques is a purely textual creation, the product rather than the producer of the words he writes. Barthes's comments in "The Death of the Author" on modern literature's substitution of a "scriptor" for an author apply without adaptation to Julien's effacement during his transcription of the letters which are to make his fortune: "The modern scriptor is born simultaneously with the text, is in no way equipped with a being preceding or exceeding the writing, is not the subject with the book as predicate; there is no other time than that of the enunciation, and every text is eternally written *here and now*" (145). Identical to Barthes's modernist achievements, Julien's letters are pure inscription without expression, pure textuality without reference, pure writing without authorship.

In *La Carte postale*, Jacques Derrida uses correspondence's necessary detachment from its author and recipient to exemplify writing's escape from origins, destinations, and reference. Julien's correspondence with Mme de Fervaques is in this sense an exemplary Derridean moment. Korasoff's friend Kalisky has his letters copied before delivering them to his Quaker. Korasoff receives a copy of the copy, Julien a copy of the copy of the copy, Mme de Fervaques a copy of the copy of the copy of the copy. Moreover, even the "original" letters have no more referential value than their multiple reproductions. Not only did Kalisky make no effort to write what he actually felt, he also recognized that writing's principal purpose is simply to exist as writing: "The first forty letters were intended only to secure forgiveness for the daring decision to write" (*Le Rouge et le noir*, 409). The act that produces the chevalier de la Vernaye is total submission to words that represent a void.

In another Derridean twist, the episode with Mme de Fervaques makes speech as unreliable as writing. Everything Julien says to the maréchale is actually intended for Mathilde, nothing he says to Mathilde represents anything he actually feels. Julien's first step toward winning Mme de Fervaques's heart is to speak in such a way that London, Paris, and all other words become interchangeable and indistinguishable. "He grew so animated that Mme de Fervaques could no longer understand what he was saying. This was a first step forward" (405). The gibberish addressed to Mme de Fervaques reaches Mathilde, its alternate destination, only on condition that whatever remains comprehensible be obviously untrue: " 'The more what I say is false, the more she'll like me,' thought Julien" (408). This insight is among the novel's most succinct statements of the inverse correlation between language's referential validity and performative force in Restoration society. In order for words to do something, they must categorically refuse to say anything.

When writing to Mme de Fervaques, Julien is an unresistant medium through which language passes as if there were no one there. When speaking to Mathilde, his absence is just as pure. The emotions he feels for Mathilde are so intense that their description slips into the Romantic rhetoric Stendhal spent much of his life trying to keep out of his prose; for example, Julien is "penetrated by love to the most intimate recesses of his heart. Never had he worshipped her to such an extent" (420). Despite this fervor, however, Julien speaks as if he felt nothing at all. He conquers Mathilde "while listening to the sound of the empty words his mouth was saying as he would have listened to an alien noise" (420). The empty sounds coming from his mouth are the oral equivalent of the empty letters copied by his hand. Both estrange language from the circumstances in which it is produced and from the subjectivity of its producer. Whether seducing in Paris or when reciting the Bible in Verrières, the language that works is language that abnegates the referential function.

Yet Mme de Fervaques instantaneously sees through Julien's letters to an indubitable, incontrovertible referent. She reads what he writes as the direct manifestation of solid identity which permits no misinterpretation. "It's impossible not to perceive devotion, extreme seriousness, and much conviction in the prose of this young priest; he will display the gentle virtue of Massillon" (407). The assurance with which Mme de Fervaques discerns reality where there is none may be connected to her need for others to do for her what she does for Julien. At the summit of a community based on contempt for bourgeois values, she owes her position to bourgeois activity. As a result, she too requires signs that create identity instead of denoting it. "Her whole life seemed to have no object other than to make everyone forget that she was the daughter of an *industrialist*" (396). "Up to the time she saw Julien, Mme de Fervaques's greatest pleasure had been to write the word *maréchale* beside her name" (415). The italics are Stendhal's, and the two italicized words are in contrary relation to the world. *Industrialist* names reality, *maréchale* its social representation, and Mme de Fervaques's lifelong struggle is to assure that the latter transcends the former. When she immediately penetrates Julien's letters to grasp the concrete substance they depict, she replicates the process through which she wants her fellows to identify her. Writing *maréchale* is her equivalent to Julien copying Kalisky. Both exercises in the free play of signifiers become referentially unimpeachable because their readers assume them to be so.

In Derrida's *La Carte postale*, the correspondent brought into being through a collection of verbal signs dissolves through the same semiotic interaction that gave him life. In Stendhal's *Le Rouge et le noir*, signs' products are incomparably more solid. Although writing *maréchale* beside her name is Mme de Fervaques's private amusement, public performance of the same fatuous enterprise creates the powerful woman who distributes the most important positions in the Church of France. Analogously, Julien's correspondence with the maréchale exemplifies what Barthes discussed in "Death of the Author," written documents irrevocably severed from any preexisting personality. In conversation with Mathilde, while listening to the words that come from his mouth as if they came from somewhere far away, Julien proclaims that the speaker is as dead as the author. But Mme de Fervaques falls in love with the writer of the borrowed letters, Mathilde with the speaker of the alien words. To designate the entity that exists solely within writing, Barthes invents a neologism undefiled by previous use to refer to reality, *scriptor*. To designate the human being whose linguistic production is followed by full integration into the world, Stendhal chooses a name with daunting referential force, M. le chevalier de la Vernaye. As Mathilde understood at the duc de Retz's ball, the emptiness prior to declaration of social identity is irrelevant to the fullness that follows it. Like Louis XVII, the chevalier de la Vernaye acquires historical substance at the same time he attains linguistic form.

The distinction between Barthes's scriptor and Stendhal's chevalier—not what precedes writing but what succeeds it—is analogous to the difference between realist and modernist fiction. Realism uses words to convey the impression of reality, modernism to convey the impression of words. Although neither genre escapes the iron law of representation, according to which the representing medium inevitably dominates the thing represented, realism enacts the fact that collective conventions can effectively abolish the distance between reality and representation. In *Du Pape*, immunity from accusations of error is in practice exactly the same thing as infallibility. In *Le Rouge et le noir*, immunity from accusations of falsehood is in practice exactly the same thing as truth. Stendhal's invention of Julien Sorel, society's invention of the chevalier de la Vernaye, and Restoration history's invention of Louis XVII are comparably persuasive demonstrations that verbal production and social reality are in no sense mutually exclusive.

All of Julien's many identities have a double textual character. At first unfounded, ungrounded, and void, they nevertheless become founding, grounding, and complete when a collectivity accepts the names given them as authentically referential. It is the second moment in this sequence that distinguishes realism from the modernist genres that followed it and leads to an intriguing question. If realist narrative is consistently concerned with the historically specific conventions that make signs appear to refer, is there a sense in which realism—like modernism—embodies the verbal operations it also represents? Modernist experiments confound the reader with words while showing characters universally confounded with words. Does realist fiction analogously make words do for the reader what they do for *its* characters, assume referential authority while simultaneously denying that this authority is based on reference?

In the case of *Le Rouge et le noir*, the answer is an unqualified yes. Readers of this novel must begin by going through a process identical to that which produces the duc de Chaulnes's younger son, the blatant display of signs' unqualified arbitrariness. Yet Stendhal's readers, like his characters, immediately learn that signs' arbitrariness is immaterial to their representational power. What precedes the realist discourse of *Le Rouge et le noir?* Not only the facts of the Restoration but also a triple demonstration that the connection between discourse and facts is never reliable. The novel's title and its first two epigraphs detach language from reality as insistently as Julien's letters to Mme de Fervaques and his speech to Mathilde. That a quintessentially representational novel follows these introductory instances of antirepresentational dissemination makes the novel as a whole a perfect figure for its major social theme: reference, never immanent to language itself, is always reliable within the confines of a language community.

"Le rouge et le noir" denotes nothing. Or rather it denotes everything its readers want it to. Like the color of Julien's suits, the color of his novel has no referent until the addressee supplies one. Like the marquis de la Mole, we readers have obligingly supplied referents and thus have assured that the red and the black convey a sense as firm as the blue. Stendhal's critics have for a century and a half been doing for the title given to his novel precisely what his characters do for the titles given to them, that is, attach a representational function to words that have none. "Red" and "black" have been taken to refer to the army and the Church, political liberalism and ecclesiastical reaction, and the colors on a roulette wheel with the same groundless certainty displayed when society ratifies the chevalier de Beauvoisis's decision that Julien Sorel is the illegitimate son of one of the marquis de la Mole's noble friends. Critic Henri Martineau's announcement of what the title really means has the depth of conviction apparent when Beauvoisis's friends defend the legitimacy of his duel. In both cases, a fact passes even though it is demonstrably not a fact. "The red indicates Julien's republicanism as the black designates ecclesiastical circles. There can be no more obscurity except for those who enjoy surrounding classic works with clouds that they themselves produce for the pleasure of bursting through them" (346). To attach so

unequivocal a meaning to so equivocal a title does *for* the text
what is repeatedly done *in* it, interpret words as the names of
things when they are actually nothing more than the names of
words. The truth of "le rouge et le noir," as of *Le Rouge et le
noir*, is that the truth of language is whatever its users attribute
to it.

The novel's epigraph extends the demonstration to the truth
of truth. "*La vérité, l'âpre vérité*. Danton" is the same kind of
self-deconstructing syntagm as André Breton's "soluble fish,"
for Danton never said "La vérité, l'âpre vérité." The bitter truth
is consequently that there is no such thing as truth if we take
the word to mean objective facts independent of their representation. Like Stendhal's title, his epigraph has become in critical
writings the opposite of what it is in his text. The truth the
novel will express is not language's referential but its performative force.

After a nonreferential title and an antireferential epigraph,
the text proper begins by detaching language from meaning as
well as reference. The epigraph to Chapter 1, Part I of *Le Rouge
et le noir* is

> Put thousands together
> Less bad,
> But the cage less gay.
> HOBBES

Not only did Hobbes never say any such thing, but this English
quotation means that Stendhal's monolingual readers reach his
text across mysterious, impenetrable foreign words. Bilingual
readers are no better off. What "Hobbes" said is as senseless
to native speakers of English as to those who know no English
at all. Put thousands of what together? Does "less bad" refer
to the thousands or to their coming together? What kind of
cage is it, and what is less bad about its being less gay? Like
the novel's title, the epigraph to its first chapter conveys no
meaning except what its readers create for it.

The necessity of producing its meaning may help explain why

the first chapter's epigraph is printed as a poetic excerpt when Hobbes never wrote poetry. Etymologically and teleologically, poetry is verbal creation rather than verbal reference. After a title designating nothing and an apostrophe to truth with an untrue attribution, *Le Rouge et le noir* gives language the form canonically associated with autonomous verbal expression. Stendhal opens his novel with three different instances of a linguistic form that repels all efforts to determine its origin, its purpose, and its sense.

Then comes language that has stood as a faithful description of reality for more than a hundred and fifty years. "Put thousands together Less bad, But the cage less gay. HOBBES" segues into "The small village of Verrières could pass for one of the prettiest in Franche Comté" and the classic realist narrative of human experience in a precise sociohistorical milieu. A tripartite antirepresentational exercise prepares the novel that inaugurated the golden age of Western literature's exemplary representational form; three demonstrations that "realist literature" is a contradiction in terms introduce five hundred pages in which realist literature became a historical fact.

Le Rouge et le noir thus does for itself just what it does for Julien and the society in which he lives; it converts farcical displays of language's irremediable alienation from reality into compelling proof that language is reality's direct and unmediated expression. Madame de Fervaques reads Kalisky's letters and identifies Julien with Massillon, Stendhal's critics read *Le Rouge et le noir* and identify Julien with Antoine Berthet. The grounds for the identifications are unimportant, what matters is that in each case an actual human being emerges from words that obviously contain no such thing. Danton did not say "La vérité, l'âpre vérité," 1814 was not the nineteenth year of Louis XVIII's reign; nevertheless, scholastic manuals such as P.-G. Castex and P. Surer's confidently use Stendhal's epigraph to state the essence of his novelistic accomplishment and Louis XVIII got away with his idiosyncratic counting practices. The great mimetic achievement of *Le Rouge et le noir* is its reproduction of the great mimetic achievement of the Restoration, establishing the sensation of extrasemiotic reality through signs that have no descriptive value of any kind.

The most nearly explicit articulation of the novel's *mise en abîme* of its own spurious representationality comes at the end of the ascendant phase of its protagonist's career. When Julien Sorel, a purely verbal creation, becomes the chevalier de la Vernaye, a purely verbal creation, he understands his success as the conclusion of a novel: " 'After all," he thought, 'my novel is over, and it's due to me alone' " (442). Like the most skillful of realist authors, Julien has taken empty words and produced the plenitude of a being accepted as real by all his readers. His novel has ended because the realist illusion has triumphed.

The red, the black, and the Restoration thus name not a work of fiction and its actual referent but a single, unitary vision of how sense is made. The historical semantics of realist fiction represents a universe in which meaning—to return to Barthes's "Death of the Author"—does not precede but does exceed the signs expressing it. The Restoration itself was based on a series of verbal strategies preceded by twenty-five years of turbulent demonstrations that they could be nothing more than exercises in autotelic textuality. But those strategies worked. The Restoration exceeded its originative assertion that the Revolution and Empire were unconnected to the reality of France and acquired a solid place in history. The multiple ways in which the peasant Julien Sorel acquires a solid place in aristocratic society are so many commentaries on a world in which solidity could be nothing more than a matter of convention. Canonical readings of Julien's novel make it clear that solidity and convention have continued to form our most basic understanding of what is real in realism.

No two understandings of the real in realism could be more contradictory than those in Erich Auerbach's *Mimesis* and Roman Jakobson's "On Realism in Art." For Jakobson, realism and the real are mutually exclusive. What we call realist art is not a representation of reality but a refusal of previous representations that have become too obviously artificial. Whenever a given arrangement of semiotic material appears referential, we can be sure that the appearance depends solely on a deviation from previous arrangements of semiotic material. If realism actually depicted the extraliterary universe, its form would be stable and unvarying. In fact, its form varies dramatically and incessantly. Every representation hailed for being true to life has been supplanted by an innovation representing a different truth and a different life. Every form transcending conventionality has been shown to be covert institution of different conventions. For Jakobson, the only distinguishing feature of the realist form is that it dissociates itself from the realist form that preceded it.

Mimesis summarizes its counterargument in its subtitle, *The Representation of Reality in Western Literature*, and makes its points most pertinently in the great chapter on Stendhal, Balzac, and Flaubert entitled "In the Hôtel de la Mole." Where Jakobson defines the history of realism as cyclical substitution of one set of stylistic novelties for another, Auerbach conceives Western literature as a linear development culminating in the nineteenth-century French novel. Against Jakobson's position that realism refers only to other art forms, those it refuses to copy, Auerbach identifies the dominant realist referent as history itself. One approach considers a content-free literary exercise definable solely by its antagonistic intertexts, the other addresses literary incorporation of actual human existence at a specific time and in a specific place. Jakobson prohibits all concern with the historical facts that Auerbach makes prerequisite to comprehension of every utterance in the realist corpus.

Auerbach summarizes his position in his introductory comments on a conversation between Julien and the abbé Pirard in *Le Rouge et le noir*. "What interests us in the scene is this: it would be almost incomprehensible without a most accurate and detailed knowledge of the political situation, the social stratification, and the economic circumstances of a perfectly definite historical moment, namely, that in which France found itself just before the July Revolution; accordingly, the novel bears the subtitle, *Chronique de 1830*" (455).

Jakobson takes the real out of realism; Auerbach makes a

"most accurate and detailed knowledge" of the real the sine qua non of decoding a realist text. The dichotomy is stark, and it would be futile to try to explain it away altogether. I nevertheless want to argue that a speech-act perspective significantly reduces the distance between Auerbach and Jakobson, which is to say between traditional and antitraditional definitions of the realist project. Austin's insistence on the importance of conventions in human existence, obviously applicable to Jakobson's realism, is in fact also directly relevant to Auerbach's reality.

The principal characteristic of the realist constative is its production of a fact from invocation of the semiotic forms conventionally associated with factuality, and it is precisely this kind of productive activity that Auerbach invokes to define Stendhal's Restoration: "The inadequately implemented attempt which the Bourbon regime made to restore conditions long since made obsolete by events, creates, among its adherents in the official and ruling classes, an atmosphere of pure convention. ... These people are conscious that they no longer themselves believe in the thing they represent" (456). Conditions perpetuated despite having been made obsolete by events, representation divorced from belief in the thing represented—Auerbach's account of the traits defining Stendhal's characters universalizes the performative identity of Louis XVII and the chevalier de la Vernaye. A representation's validity is determined not by its fidelity to a referent but by the quintessentially speech-act criterion of conformity to "an atmosphere of pure convention."

Pure convention is equally prominent in Auerbach's reading of the passage that he presents as typifying the great achievement of *Le Rouge et le noir*, the introduction of mature fictional mimesis into the canon of Western literature. Julien's conversation with the abbé Pirard is about boredom and its effects, not about the Restoration and its events. The words Auerbach defines as incomprehensible without precise knowledge of "the political situation, the social stratification, and the economic circumstances of a perfectly definite historical moment" are almost devoid of political, social, economic, and historical content. Rather than one of the many passages in Stendhal's novel that allude directly to a historical referent, Auerbach begins his chapter on the realist achievement by explicating a text in which historical reference is astonishingly oblique. The perfectly definite historical moment depends for its perfect definition on exactly the same interpretive gestures responsible for Jakobson's realism.

Furthermore, Auerbach's description of how Stendhal experienced the reality he fictionalized has striking affinities with Jakobson's description of how readers determine that art is realistic. In Auerbach's understanding, Stendhal was able to produce the "entirely new and highly significant phenomenon" (458) of a literary form adequately incorporating historical fact because he perceived all historical solidity slipping away. Auerbach's extended discussion of Stendhal's sensitivity to social reality takes as its leitmotif reality's ephemeral nature. The French Revolution produced not a referent to be represented but a series of representations that never managed to make themselves appear legitimate. If Stendhal invented the literary genre best suited to depicting humanity's social nature, it was because he was the first major novelist of whom it could so confidently be said that "the social world around him became a problem" (461). Realist representation is not that in which society is most completely reproduced but that in which social representations are most emphatically problematized.

Here is Auerbach on the staggering compression of time effected by the French Revolution and so vividly experienced at certain moments of Stendhal's biography that "modern consciousness of reality began to find literary form for the first time precisely in Henri Beyle of Grenoble" (459). The vastly accelerated historical tempo produced by the Revolution

> abrogates or renders powerless the entire social structure of orders and categories previously held valid; the tempo of the changes demands a perpetual and extremely difficult effort toward inner adaptation and produces intense concomitant crises. He who would account to himself for his real life and his place in human society is obliged to do so upon a far wider practical foundation and in a far larger context than before, and to be continually

conscious that the social base upon which he lives is not constant for a moment but is perpetually changing through convulsions of the most various kinds. [459]

Orders and categories previously held valid dissolve into nothingness, the social base on which all sensation of reality depends is perpetually and convulsively shifting. In Marx's words, all that is solid melts into air; in Voloshinov's, yesterday's truth is today's lie. *Mimesis* grounds its vision of the seminal moment in literary representation of reality in Stendhal's forced recognition that no reality is durable enough to permit its repesentations to be objectively validated.

The mutant orders and categories that Auerbach ascribes to reality are directly analogous to those Jakobson ascribes to realism. Jakobson considers realism a "social fact" ("On Realism in Art," 42) that changes with the society responsible for its factuality. Auerbach views life as positioned on a "social base" that is "not constant for a moment but is perpetually changing through convulsions of the most various kinds." For Jakobson, realism's "concrete content...is extremely relative" (42). For Auerbach, reality's concrete content is the same. Alike in defining the realist enterprise as a set of conventional procedures having conventional effect, Jakobson and Auerbach differ in that the former associates the relativity of realism with that of reality and the latter confines his remarks to the conventions that perform the real in its artistic forms alone.

The distance between *Mimesis* and naive concepts of mimesis is implicit in the difference between Auerbach's German subtitle and Willard Trask's translation of it. What was in the original *dargestellte Wirklicheit*—represented reality— became in English "representation of reality." The reality that must be represented to be real is the core of Austin's constative, whereas the suggestion in Trask's translation is that reality and representation are disparate. That disparity is Jakobson's primary target in "On Realism in Art," but Auerbach's reading of Stendhal does not permit reality to stand apart from the conventions of its performance. Like the National Assembly of 1789, like Sarrasine's castrato, like Rastignac and Louis XVII, the characters of *Le Rouge et le noir* exist for Auerbach by virtue of the forms of their representation. Their reality is the same "social fact" that Jakobson sees in the existence of the realist form.

In an early formulation of what Barthes would call the reality effect, Jakobson attributes the sensation that physical facts are present in the text to realism's inclusion of details considered unworthy of mention in earlier works. The realism chapter in *Mimesis* discusses physical facts in its analysis of the introduction of Mme Vauquer in *Le Père Goriot*, an analysis that begins by discussing Balzac's representation of the material world as if materiality were indeed one of fiction's components. "The entire description, so far as we have yet considered it, is directed to the mimetic imagination of the reader, to his memory-pictures of similar persons and similar milieux which he may have seen" (471). Jakobson's most telling point is that fictional descriptions are never actually directed to a reader's memory-pictures and appear so only because they diverge from previously processed memory-texts. At this stage, Auerbach's definition of Balzacian mimesis seems to entail faith in a permanent, fixed reality shared by author and reader across the centuries.

But the key phrase in Auerbach's assessment is "so far as we have yet considered it." Appeal to memory-pictures is but a first step toward constitution of realist prose, for the objects comprising Mme Vauquer's world take their sense from sociohistorical conventions, from the "sociological and ethical significance of furniture and clothing" (471) that makes such objects into signs.

[Balzac] not only, like Stendhal, places the human beings whose destiny he is seriously relating, in their precisely defined historical and social setting, but also conceives this connection as a necessary one: to him every milieu becomes a moral and physical atmosphere which impregnates the landscape, the dwelling, furniture, implements, clothing, physique, character, surroundings, ideas, activities, and fates of men, and at the same time the general historical situation reappears as a total atmosphere which envelops all its several milieux. [473]

No detail is unessential when every detail is impregnated with the significance assigned it by a sociological and historical unit. As a corollary, no detail stands on its own because all are connected to the conventions that make a sociological unit itself. "In this precisely defined historical and social setting," the components of the material world are also the effects of conventional procedures.

The move from step one to step two in Auerbach's analysis of Mme Vauquer's introduction consequently amounts to repudiation of step one. Like human beings, physical objects take their presence from the conventions underlying their designation, not from memory-pictures of nonconventional reality.

Mimesis continues its discussion of Balzac by contrasting the represented reality of *Le Père Goriot* to the theory made responsible for it in the *Avant-propos* to the *Comédie humaine*. According to Balzac's own explanation of his novels, their dominant compositional principle is the analogy between Nature and society. From Auerbach's historicist position, no analogy could be more misleading. Whereas Nature is a given, society is perpetual self-transformation. *Mimesis* argues that, while Balzac's novels incorporate this distinction as central to their textual organization, his theory collapses it. As a result, the *Avant-propos* can be taken seriously only if it is always subject to refutation by the practice it is supposed to explain. "The epitomizing sentence reads: 'The social State has risks which Nature does not permit herself, for it is Nature plus Society.' Inaccurate and macroscopic as this passage is, badly as it suffers from the *proton pseudos* of the underlying comparison, it yet contains an instinctive historical insight ('customs, clothing, modes of speech, houses...change in accordance with civilizations')" (476). In Auerbach's view, Balzac's theoretical grasp of the reality he was representing was vitiated when he assimilated it to the permanence of the natural world. To privilege Nature as a model for understanding human existence is to posit a referent independent of the socialized function responsible for every component of historicist reality.

A disparaging allusion to Balzac's pop Platonism encapsulates Auerbach's quarrel with a reality divorced from a historical matrix. In the *Avant-propos,* "the model-concept, the principle 'animal' or 'man,' is not taken as immanent but, so to speak, as a real Platonic idea. The various genera and species are only *formes extérieures;* furthermore, they are themselves given not as changing within the course of history but as fixed (a soldier, a workman, etc., like a lion, an ass)" (475). Identical to constative truth, historicist identity cannot be conceptualized apart from a social environment. Identical to Jakobson's realism, Auerbach's reality is meaningless if we imagine it "not as changing within the course of history but as fixed." Nature, Platonic ideals, the referent, and autonomous reality are alien to Auerbach's vision of what is represented in the literary form inaugurated by Balzac and Stendhal.

How does Auerbach reconcile this thoroughly contextualized reality with his concomitant assertions that nineteenth-century French realism developed a means for depicting the world as, in Leopold von Ranke's canonical historicist credo, it really was? The contention here is that he does not, that efforts to define the realist achievement as faithful depiction of what Auerbach repeatedly calls "reality as given" (463, 466, 468, and so on) are finally not convincing. Comparing the theory and practice of *Mimesis* is analogous to comparing the theory and practice of the *Comédie humaine.* In both cases, theoretical statements are radically dissonant from the discursive practice they are supposed to explain. Interspersed among the analyses of realism in *Mimesis,* historicist axioms about reality as given are as incongruous as Balzac's appeal to Nature as the model for his representation of society.

The theory/practice disjuncture in *Mimesis* has repeatedly struck Auerbach's readers. Eckhard Höfner's *Literarität und Realität* takes the Jakobson/Auerbach dichotomy as its point of departure and argues that only Jakobson furnishes a conceptually valid frame for analyzing nineteenth-century realism. Höfner is careful, however, to specify that his assessment of Auerbach addresses the theory alone; the practice is another matter altogether. "The richness of insight, the excellence of the many striking interpretations Auerbach provides, will not be taken into account" (16; my translation).

In his introduction to *The Political Unconscious*, Fredric Jameson gives a more general assessment of the disparity between the undoubted value of Auerbach's criticism and the highly questionable value of its points of departure.

> Of literary history today we may observe that its task is at one with that proposed by Louis Althusser for historiography in general: not to elaborate some achieved and lifelike simulacrum of its supposed object, but rather to "produce" the latter's "concept." This is indeed what the greatest modern or modernizing literary histories—such as Erich Auerbach's *Mimesis*—have sought to do in their critical practice, if not in their theory. [12]

Jameson's inclusion of Auerbach within the project of Althusserian historiography is especially provocative, for one of Althusser's tenets is the irrelevance of historicism to serious social inquiry. Whereas Auerbach writes as if calling a novel "thoroughly historicistic" (480) is the highest praise, Jameson's evaluation denies that historicism contributes meaningfully to Auerbach's understanding of what novels actually say. As "produced" in the critical essays of *Mimesis*, realism repels historicist categories.

The function of footnotes can help categorize the distance between Auerbach and historicist criticism in general. When a novel is, as Auerbach says of *Le Rouge et le noir*, incomprehensible without most accurate and detailed information about its setting, it is normally because its words convey a historicized sense that cannot be inferred from their context. *Ultra* and *congregation* are two of countless such words in *Le Rouge et le noir*. Footnotes could furnish their historically determinate sense by describing how those words were used by Stendhal's contemporaries. The hermeneutic route would lead from extratextual facts to the text itself.

That is of course the route closed off by the axioms dominating both the contemporary human sciences and Jakobson's 1921 "On Realism in Art." But the essential point is that this route is not Auerbach's and is not relevant to the discussion of Julien Sorel's boredom in *Mimesis*. *Boredom* and *congregation* make vastly different hermeneutic demands. A footnote to the latter might usefully say that it was "a semisecret politico-religious organization to which immense power was attributed during the Restoration." But it is hard to imagine an editor feeling compelled to footnote *boredom* as "a debilitating sensation of vacuousness and lack of purpose widely experienced just before the July Revolution."

Auerbach, however, gives something very like that improbable footnote: "We are confronted, in [characters'] boredom, by a phenomenon politically and ideologically characteristic of the Restoration period" (456). In my imaginary footnote to *congregation*, the Restoration *precedes* novelistic iteration of one of its words. In Auerbach's commentary on *boredom*, the Restoration *proceeds* from a word communicating perfectly well without it. This type of critical performance is far indeed from reality as given.

In distinction to critics who, like Martineau, attribute indubitable referential solidity to their conventional interpretations of *rouge*, *noir*, and *Le Rouge et le noir*, Auerbach illustrates the Althusserian project of producing his object's concept by bringing his critical practice into harmony with his delineation of Stendhal's novelistic universe. The critic represents the novelist by deriving historical specificity from textual interpretation rather than the reverse. The novelist represents the Restoration by deriving historical solidity from social semiotics rather than the reverse. Outrageous as the foreclosure of meaning in Auerbach's definition of boredom is, it gets quite a legitimate punch from its application to novelistic representation of a society that also assigns precise referential value to terms that have none. In *Le Rouge et le noir*, a nineteenth-century state acts as if the eighteenth century had not ended, collectively submerges substance under form, collectively collapses referents into conventions. The critic does for *boredom* what characters do for *chevalier de la Vernaye:* create an unimpeachable fact from an echoing emptiness. In the terms of Barthes's reality effect, what Stendhal chronicles is not the Restoration but the Restoration effect. At issue is not a referent but a performance, and Auerbach interprets accordingly.

But history's conventionality in no way makes it insubstantial. Although Stendhal's characters no longer believe in the thing they represent, their combined representation creates the only reality available to them. Although language is mendacious to the point of madness, its users' unanimous concurrence suffices to make it unimpeachable. The assurance with which Auerbach produces a perfectly definite historical moment from a historically indefinite verbal construct matches that with which Stendhal's characters produce a perfectly awesome historical force from their passive reiteration of obsolete language. The subject of Stendhal's fiction is society as fiction, that of Auerbach's analysis the represented reality of represented reality.

In a strong Derridean critique of *Mimesis*, David Carroll writes: "*Mimesis* argues that the real exists outside of and prior to its representation—it is the source of its representation.... Auerbach demands that the realist get back to the 'real itself' before its distortion" (12). Although valid for historicist programmatics, that summary is at odds with the concept of realism actually produced by Auerbach's analysis of Stendhal. Characters immersed in an atmosphere of pure convention forestall any possibility of moving beyond convention to seize reality at its source. What Carroll sees as Auerbach's failure to defend his precepts can also be understood as his success in disencumbering his analysis from his historicism.

Carroll's summary of what historicism cannot say is a perfect synopsis of what Auerbach does say about the represented reality of *Le Rouge et le noir*.

The process of representation has begun from the start, before the institution of the real as a presence—in this sense, the "real in itself" is always-already representation.

The real, then, which according to the principles of *Mimesis* should be the *origin* of Auerbach's essays... becomes a product of Auerbach's own system—not present in itself, the real exists only as it is (re)constructed by Auerbach from its traces in the various texts he analyzes. [12]

Besides encapsulating precisely what Auerbach says about Stendhal's characters (the real as presence is the effect of representation), this passage also makes explicit what is implicit in Auerbach's choice of an ahistorical passage to exemplify the historical meaning of *Le Rouge et le noir*, the (re)construction of the real from a text in which its traces are virtually indiscernible. With no pretense of doing anything else, *Mimesis* institutes 1830 as a presence in a passage that affords no objective ground for doing so. From that arbitrary beginning, Auerbach goes on to argue that Stendhal's 1830 is the same as his own, always-already representation, verbal depiction of a verbal depiction. The novel and its analysis make the same point. Meaning is a performance, but the performance's enabling conventions suffice to make it appear referential.

Carroll's critique of *Mimesis* is like Barthes's critique of Balzacian mimesis. Both dismissals assume a will to reference when their objects actually supplant the referent with the constative. In contrast to positivist literary historians, Auerbach's concern is *represented* reality. In contrast to recent literary theory, his concern is represented *reality*. The essays expounding that parity of emphasis are a model application of the vision that Austin codified by defining constative expression.

5

Performance and Class
in the Month of Germinal

The standard literary-manual definition of the traits distinguishing realism from naturalism—Balzac and Stendhal from
Zola—is the naturalist preoccupation with details for their own
sake. The harsh assessment of Zola's style in Gustave Lanson
and Paul Tuffrau's history of French literature typifies a formerly
unchallenged attitude: "The tendency toward descriptive am-
plification is quite marked, and the abundance of detail is a
singular encumbrance in this style, already monotonous. . . .
Everything becomes matter, weighty and powerful like matter"
(686; my translation). In terms of the distinction between constative and referential nomenclature, Zola is for Lanson and
Tuffrau the quintessence of referentiality. Details enter his texts
in the transparent language of the names for things, heavy and
obtrusive as the things themselves.

In his essays "Narrate or Describe?" and "The Zola Centenary," Gyorgy Lukács joins Lanson in rejecting unmotivated naturalist description as a failed continuation of the
fully integrated description characteristic of serious realism.
Despite the immense distance between Lanson's and Lukács's systems of critical values, both men concur that Zola's details strike a deadly blow against the aesthetics of
meaningful fiction. A celebrated passage from the "Zola
Centenary" essay in *Studies in European Realism* summarizes Lukács's opinion.

Perhaps no one has painted more colorfully and suggestively the outer trappings of modern life.

But only the *outer* trappings.

They form a gigantic backdrop in front of which tiny, haphazard people move to and fro and live their haphazard lives. Zola could never achieve what the truly great realists Balzac, Tolstoy or Dickens accomplished: to present social institutions as human relationships and social objects as the vehicle of such relationships. Man and his surroundings are always sharply divided in all Zola's works. [92–93]

To present objects as the vehicle of human relationships and to present those relationships as the form taken in the novel by social institutions: in Austin's language, that imperative becomes constative designation of objects as the conventional effect of conventional procedures. In both formulations, Zola's error is to attempt novelistic reference without attending to the collective assumptions that make any referent a constituent of collective consciousness.

Lukács's critique of Zola's atomistic details has a dual thrust. On the one hand, objects and events appear detached from the web of human relationships that alone can ground authentically realist art. On the other hand, those reified details are textually isolated elements without organic connection to the other constituents of the work in which they appear. The philosophical shortcoming responsible for "the direct, mechanical mirroring of the humdrum reality of capitalism" (*Studies in European Realism*, 93) is consonant with the literary shortcoming of a form in which elements "act without a pattern, either merely side by side or else in completely chaotic fashion" (91). The realist constative requires names that designate reality by virtue of a network of textual conventions corresponding to the network of social conventions foregrounded in Austin's Rule A.1. Lukács's and Lanson's critiques situate Zola's naturalism below both achievements of the realist constative. Naturalist names bear semantic force only by virtue of the material substance of what they designate, and any such nomenclature is by definition an interloper in the textual construct that incorporates it. Zola's descriptive style is for Lukács a perfect example of what Barthes called "the *direct* collusion of a referent and a signifier" ("L'Effet de réel," 88).

I want to contest Lukács's assumption by examining what happens to one group of names for things in the section of *Germinal* that narrates the striking miners' visit to Hennebeau's house for the first articulation of their grievances. Already nervous about the unaccustomed role of making demands instead of executing them, the miners are further intimidated by the imposing objects that surround them in the room where they are told to wait for Hennebeau's arrival. The text's description of their discomfort includes a long list of the things that intensify their malaise, a list that could serve as a model of unrelievedly referential discourse. In the following quotation, I emphasize the section of the description most illustrative of Lanson's opinion that Zola's style is as heavy and awkward as the matter it evokes with such studied determination.

> [Les mineurs] roulaient leurs casquettes entre les doigts, ils jetaient des regards obliques sur le mobilier, une de ces confusions de tous les styles, que le goût de l'antiquaille a mises à la mode: *des fauteuils Henri II, des chaises Louis XV, un cabinet italien du dix-septième siècle, un contador espagnol du quinzième, et un devant d'autel pour le lambrequin de la cheminée, et des chamarres d'anciennes chasubles réappliquées sur les portières.* Ces vieux ors, ces vieilles soies aux tons fauves, tout ce luxe de chapelle, les avait saisis d'un malaise respectueux. Les tapis d'Orient semblaient les lier aux pieds de leur haute laine.

> [The miners] were fingering the caps held before them and looking sideways at the furniture, one of those confused mixtures of all styles that the taste for everything antique had made fashionable: *Henri II armchairs, Louis XV straight chairs, a seventeenth-century Italian cabinet, a fifteenth-century Spanish contador, and an altar-front over the mantel, and bright embroidery from old chasubles attached to the drapery.* This old gold, these old bright silks, all this chapel-like luxury held them in the grip of a respectful discomfort. The Oriental rugs seemed to tie their feet down with high wool pile. [1318–19; all translations from Zola are my own]

One of Lukács's strictures, that Zola does not represent social objects as the vehicle of human relationships, is immediately and decisively refuted by this passage. The *things* in his living room are Hennebeau's principal weapons in his struggle against the *humans* there, the struggle that also plays itself out in every other representation of objects in *Germinal*. Far from being "only the *outer* trappings" of life in a class society, Hennebeau's furnishings are crucial to the inner being of their owner and of his antagonists. Objects' textual presence is the consequence of their ideological value, and both sides in the social conflict experience their selfhood in starkly ideological form.

In the quoted passage, objects enter the text through the miners' uncomfortable perception of that which makes their inferiority palpable. This subject-object reversal leads first to my italicized list of objects divorced from humans, then to the grammatical subordination of people to things in the final sentences' use of objects as agents and humans as the passive recipients of their action: "this chapel-like luxury held them in the grip.... The Oriental rugs seemed to tie their feet down." For Lukács, "man and his surroundings are always sharply divided in all Zola's works." Yet the passage here is typical of all Zola's works in that the isolation of surroundings in the precise, static description of Hennebeau's furniture is crucial to the dynamic enactment of a social structure informing every constituent of textual organization. When, as in the emphasized passage, objects stand on their own in a syntagm without verbs and a universe without motion, they do so through the connivance of a society without change and a hierarchy without cracks, "weighty and powerful like matter."

There is thus a first level on which Zola's style seems fully to exemplify the features identifying constative rather than referential discourse. The points at which names seem most exclusively referential is also the point at which their textual function is most thoroughly socialized. Hennebeau's possessions display the stolid inertia of things in themselves because the conventions governing interaction between workers and bourgeois decree that the marks of the latter's dominance produce something concrete and immutable. Things are present as things because they are also present as signs. By virtue of the protocols that make up the ideological system in which they simultaneously perform and are performed, bourgeois objects manifest the solidity of the bourgeois world. When workers are in their place, proper nominative procedures admit no suggestion that objects can be displaced.

The corollary is apparent. If the conventions making objects objective fail to impose their authority, the objects themselves should lose their command of the language naming them. Furthermore, if social conventions are disrupted only when social organization is disturbed, textual play with the material world ought in principle to manifest attacks on the assigned functions of society's human constituents. Such attacks are of course *Germinal*'s primary topic; the seriousness with which the novel represents economic conflict has as its stylistic consequence the spectacle of naturalist discourse in discomfiture. When classes collide in *Germinal*, objective language undergoes remarkable vicissitudes, as Hennebeau's furniture demonstrates with special clarity.

The first allusion to the antiques in the room where the strikers state their case comes while Hennebeau is still with his luncheon guests, discussing the unexpected turn of events. Workers acting as they are not supposed to act produce a set of objects that garble the message they are supposed to convey. From the perspective of a frightened bourgeoisie in the next room, the material signs of dominance vanish when dominance becomes problematic.

> C'étaient les délegués. Des portes battirent, on entendit passer un souffle d'effroi, au travers des pièces voisines . . . les pas lourds des délegués, qu'on introduisait, écrasaient à côté le tapis du salon.

> It was the delegates. Doors slammed, a startled gasp seemed to pass through the neighboring rooms . . . the heavy steps of the miners being admitted were crushing the drawing room rug. [1316]

To the intimidated miners, the carpet is tying their feet. To the intimidated bourgeois, the same carpet is being crushed to death. In both cases, politicized phenomenology prohibits any semblance of referential objectivity.

In such an environment, descriptions that appear referential must take the appearance from their political armature. The archetypically naturalist list of furnishings that precedes the miners' sensation of the rug's aggression is in fact part of the same validation of social hierarchy responsible for the rug's aggressivity. As if to illustrate, the rug and all the objects around it lose their textual presence altogether when class divisions fail to structure narrative events. Once the miners begin to speak in ways that refuse their subordination, Hennebeau's furnishings disappear along with his power. Maheu's vigorous challenges to an unjust system of labor produce this reaction from his comrades and their surroundings.

> Des voix, parmi les mineurs, s'élevèrent.
> —C'est cela... Il a dit notre idée à tous... Nous ne demandons que la raison.
> D'autres, sans parler, approuvèrent d'un hochement de tête. La pièce luxueuse avait disparu, avec ses ors et ses broderies, son entassement mystérieux d'antiquailles; et ils ne sentaient même plus le tapis, qu'ils écrasaient sous leurs chaussures lourdes.

> The miners' voices were being raised.
> "That's it... He said what we all think... We just want what's right."
> Others, without speaking, agreed by nodding their heads. The luxurious room had disappeared, with its gold and its embroidery, its mysterious accumulation of antiques; and now they didn't even feel the carpet, which they were crushing under their heavy shoes.
> [1321]

Subversive speech dissolves things as impressively as deferential attitudes magnify them. In *Germinal*, to name a thing is to invoke the conventions that make the name an act. Overturning those conventions leaves the name unspoken and the thing invisible: "The luxurious room had disappeared."

This passage from "Narrate or Describe?" summarizes Lu-kács's view of the dehumanized aesthetic accepted by novelists such as Zola.

> The autonomy of the details has varied effects, all deleterious, on the representation of men's lives. On the one hand, writers strive to describe details as completely, plasticly and picturesquely as possible; in this attempt they achieve an extraordinary artistic competence. But the description of things no longer has anything to do with the lives of characters. Not only are things described out of any context with the lives of the characters, attaining an independent significance that is not their due within the totality of the novel, but the very manner in which they are described sets them in an entirely different sphere from that in which the characters move. [132]

Description of the strikers' confrontation with Hennebeau both illustrates and refutes Lukács. The "autonomy of the details" and "independent significance of objects" are undeniable components of Zola's narrative. Yet that narrative also specifies that this autonomy is produced by collective acceptance of an ethos in which things signify more meaningfully than people. When the miners forcefully articulate their needs, objects that were autonomous become objects that cannot be seen. The "manner in which they are described" varies absolutely with the stability of the socioeconomic milieu in which objects are set.

"Narrate or Describe?" continually attacks the contention that naturalist representation of things is the literary form depicting "what capitalism does to people" (145). Lukács's argument is that such an alienated vision of the world ignores the potential of proletarian revolt, for "when this revolt is represented in literature, the still lives of descriptive mannerism vanish" (145). Although marshaled against Zola, that line of reasoning is an uncannily accurate summary of just what occurs in the episode between Hennebeau and the strikers. When they accept the values of their society, the miners appear in *Germinal* as what they are on their job, beings of less moment than the objects around them. When they rebel, the descriptive mannerism representing objects vanishes along with the objects it exalted. It is when they are most uncompromisingly depicted as things that the material constituents of the universe of *Germinal* are most decisively the effect of conventions. Zola's representation of commodity fetishism magnifies commodities to make the fetishism unmistakable. When the latter loses its power, the former lose their reality.

And this variable ontology is textually coherent because the text represents reality as a constative performance. If we accept Lukács's contention that "the still lives of descriptive mannerism" are a novelistic form of what capitalism does to people, then the capitalist constative is description striving for the highest degree of referential authority. Conversely, refusing the conventions of capitalism undermines the pretensions of reference, and objects vanish with the code enforcing their dominion. Hennebeau's antiques are like *Sarassine*'s castrato: their textual identity is purely and simply the effect of the conventions underwriting their names. The difference is that Balzac signals altered conventions by shifting from nineteenth-century Paris to eighteenth-century Rome whereas Zola effects the same shift by introducing a new consciousness rather than a new society. The essential identity remains that, in both these instances of the realist constative, names adhere to a reality only because communal conventions ratify the connection.

In *Sarrasine* and the other works discussed to this point, the prominent exemplifications of the realist constative have been human. Like the castrato, Rastignac, Goriot, Julien Sorel, and the habitués of the hôtel de la Mole take their own reality (rather than that of their possessions) from their milieu. In *Germinal*, too, constative representation of humans figures in compelling ways, and is in fact inseparable from constative representation of things. It is because a subordinate class performs its own substance that the marks of Hennebeau's superiority lose theirs. The speech acts destroying the conventional effects of one set of conventional procedures produce another set at the same time. While objects are disappearing, another representation of humanity is coming into view.

Performance of this different humanity is the work of Maheu, chosen as the miners' spokesman despite his conviction that no words of his can ever do things. Maheu's initial reaction to news of his selection as spokesman was consternation; entering Hennebeau's house accentuated his agonizing sensation of inadequacy. The man whose words are expected to change the workers' lives is the most obvious victim of the stylistically hypertrophied antiques that take away his voice. Furthermore, Hennebeau, when he finally joins the miners, magistrally continues the intimidating process begun by his furniture. The bourgeois/worker polarity takes the form of a polarity between speech and silence, for the first four components of this "dialogue" between the mine's director and its workers are the director's. Maheu screws up enough courage to talk only after an express order from his adversary. What worker's speech there is comes at the instigation of the man against whom it is directed. Moreover, when Maheu finally steps forward, Hennebeau condemns the words he wants to say even before they can be uttered: "Oh, this is bad! It's really upsetting to see you at the head of the malcontents" (1319). The mine director's reproach has the same debilitating force as his furniture, and Maheu's reaction to both is mute passivity.

But then, despite everything condemning him to silence, Maheu states workers' reality in a bourgeois setting. Repeatedly defined as unworthy of saying anything, the miners' spokesman finally rebels against the semantic structure responsible for this definition. As his discourse transforms the world and himself, an absence becomes a presence, a void a force. Textual attribution of Maheu's words map an unprecedented means for evaluating the truth of what words say and the identity of the man who says them.

Maheu écoutait, les yeux baissés. Puis il commença, la voix hésitante et sourde d'abord...Sa voix se raffermissait. Il leva les yeux, il continua, en regardant le directeur....Du reste, Maheu coupa la parole au directeur. Maintenant, il était lancé, les mots venaient tout seuls. Par moments, il s'écoutait avec surprise, comme si un étranger avait parlé en lui. C'étaient des choses amassées au fond de sa poitrine, des choses qu'il ne savait même pas là, et qui sortaient, dans un gonflement de son coeur. Il disait

leur misère à tous, le travail dur, la vie de brute, la femme et les
petits criant la faim à la maison.

Maheu was listening, his eyes lowered. Then he began, at first in
a tentative and hoarse voice...His voice was growing stronger.
He raised his eyes and went on, looking straight at the director.
...Moreover Maheu cut the director short. Now he had taken
off, the words were coming by themselves. At times he would
listen to himself with astonishment, as if a stranger had spoken
in him. These were things heaped up in his chest, things he hadn't
even known were there, and they were gushing out from his heart.
He was saying their common poverty, the hard work, the life of
a beast, the wife and kids in the house crying out from hunger.
[1319–20]

Bourgeois objects vanish because a proletarian voice is making
itself heard. The "stranger" speaking (in) Maheu is in fact a
visitor from elsewhere, from a world where the conventions for
effective verbal performance are incommensurable with those
governing conversation across class lines in the industrialized
economy of nineteenth-century France's mining region. At first,
the stranger's speech is so alien that it acts without Maheu's
agency: "the words were coming by themselves...he would
listen to himself with astonishment." But speech's power quickly
invigorates the speaker, who becomes the performer as well as
the vessel of its action.

I take the use of *dire* in "Il disait leur misère à tous" as
correlative to the constative vision of people and things informing the whole of the miners' encounter with Hennebeau. The
point of moment is not *what* Maheu says about the miners'
poverty but *that* he says it. Because words enact one class's
need, another class's things can no longer enact its superiority.
The conventions accepted by Maheu and the stranger in him
impose themselves on the rest of the group; the mark of their
success is the protean character of what they incorporate. When
the strikers again become aware of Hennebeau's furniture, what
they see is not things in themselves but theft of labor, not the
proof of class divisions but the spoils of class war. Here is how
the strikers react when Etienne takes up Maheu's demands.

Le camarade venait de réclamer leur part, au milieu de ce bien-
être; et ils recommençaient à jeter des regards obliques sur les
tentures chaudes, sur les sièges confortables, sur tout ce luxe dont
la moindre babiole aurait payé leur soupe pendant un mois.

The comrade had just laid claim to their share in the midst of all
this comfort; again they looked sideways at the warm drapery,
the soft chairs, all these sumptuous things the cheapest of which
would have bought them food for a month. [1323]

To say poverty resays as well as unsays the facts of opulence.
The strikers' performance first disassembles inherited procedures then redefines accepted effects. In the process, things that
existed in themselves come to exist for human beings, and the
language naming things is subjected to human will.

What happens when the miners act politically? They acquire
speech that itself begins to act, to act so as to destroy the impression that linguistic operations are dictated by the nature of
reality. Performative expression dissipates the referential illusion. What was most real becomes immaterial, those who were
most problematic impose their substance. The time of social
action is also the time of semantic disruption; under the threat
of political change, meaning becomes a political prize.

Voloshinov of course said the same thing in a passage already
much discussed here:

The ruling class strives to impart a supraclass, eternal character
to the ideological sign, to extinguish or drive inward the struggle
between social value judgements which occurs in it, to make the
sign uniaccentual.

In actual fact, each living ideological sign has two faces, like
Janus. Any current curse word can become a word of praise, any
current truth must inevitably sound to many other people as the
greatest lie. This *inner dialectic quality* of the sign comes out fully
in the open only in times of social crises or revolutionary changes.
[23]

When only bourgeois speech is heard in Hennebeau's house,
signs appear to emanate from their referents as the supraclass

expression of reality itself. When a different voice speaks, those referents and that reality are not discernible. As in *Marxism and the Philosophy of Language*, the validity of expression in *Germinal* varies with the prospects for social crises and revolutionary changes.

Since the strikers' visit to Hennebeau introduces only a temporary threat to continued bourgeois hegemony, however, the referential discourse of objects triumphant quickly reasserts itself. When the mine's director regains control of the meeting and the speech heard within it, the narrative voice again concentrates on the room and again validates its objects. At the end of the confrontation as at its beginning, bourgeois possessions leave workers unheard: "the heavy sound of the voices was stifled under the drapery" (1321). There follows "a confused discussion" the content of which is inconsequential. At issue is not what the words say but what they do, and the primary effect of their performance is revalidation of a sociolinguistic system organized on class lines. Maheu's voice again fails when Hennebeau's regains its smooth dominance (1323); after the miners leave, the empty room is what it was before they came, the locus of a system of values heavy and powerful as matter itself.

If *Germinal*'s performance of semiotic annihilation illustrates Voloshinov's vision of revolution's effect on signs, therefore, the same text displays in other places the unexceptionable solidity of the referential expression Voloshinov associates with social stasis. It is for this reason that Lukács's definition of naturalist description so often provides a convincing synopsis of Zola's style and is so often persuasive in indicting the style's ideological implications. Zola's descriptive techniques take on the characteristics of the realist constative by deriving reality from the society that lives it, yet those same techniques also appear to universalize social conventions by the crushing force of their textual iteration. *Germinal* contains far more instances of Voloshinov's authoritative "sign in an established, dominant ideology" than of disruptive demonstrations of signs' arbitrariness as revealed when ideologies are in turmoil.

The confrontational coexistence of referential description and its constative negation during the miners' first challenge to authority raises crucial points by virtue of the challenge's *mise en abîme* of *Germinal* as a whole. The novel begins by representing the miners' subservience to the forces running the mine, recounts their revolt, and ends with their subjugation reestablished. The chapter on Hennebeau and the militant delegates begins with workers' submission to bourgeois objects, recounts their revolt, and ends by once more making objects preeminent. As if to confirm the exemplary value of the strikers' debate, description of their departure from Hennebeau's house repeats two of the most celebrated features identifying them in the novel's introductory and closing segments. It is with "a rounded back" and a "herd-like tread" (1325) that the miners enter the text, leave it, and walk away from Hennebeau's antiques. In each version of this descriptive abasement, miners are caught in a system of signs that seems to give them no purchase on the conventions allowing those signs to bear meaning.

Yet those immobilizing signs are juxtaposed with the proof of their own fragility. Reification of workers alternates with telling assaults on the representational system that makes reification possible. The objects crushing humans vanish when humans speak in a different voice, and collective action continually suggests that truth itself can be made over. *Germinal*'s representations of people and possessions alternately display the force of the identity conventions give them and expose the fragility of every identity that requires harmonious conventions for its enactment.

The textual presence of workers, bourgeois, and things all vary with textual assessment of the seriousness of the strike's threat to social order. Maheu's verbal performance makes Hennebeau's things disappear for the same reason that it leaves Hennebeau's voice unheard, because efficacious workers' speech invalidates the preconditions for bourgeois self-definition, whether through commodities or through commands. The ultimate success of bourgeois self-definition returns commodities and commanders to their accustomed place after the strike's final collapse as after the original articulation of its purpose.

In *Confessions d'un enfant du siècle*, Musset uses a memorable phrase to express the fragility of the social system reimposed at the Bourbon Restoration. "With Napoleon dead, the powers divine and human were in fact reestablished, but belief in them no longer existed. . . . It's one thing to say, 'This could be' and quite another to say, 'This has been' " (70; my translation). In other terms, the constative identity of Restoration powers depended not only on social consensus but on a consensus that everyone knew was subject to total revocation. Imagining a new system of conventions is always subversive, but the subversion becomes intolerable when imagination becomes memory and "This could be" is "This has been." Maheu and his comrades, Etienne and his followers, are required to act for what—joining Musset to Austin—might be called the conditional constative. They fail to sustain the presence they occasionally perform because sustained performance requires conventions that could be but have not yet been. Conversely, bourgeois power is reinforced by the knowledge that it not only could be but has been and is. The social system on which power depends is challenged but not overturned, as the objects in Hennebeau's salon disappear but soon recover their materiality.

Musset goes on to describe the demystification of Restoration fetishes by collective memory that a fetish is nothing more than a thing. "And, when people spoke of the throne and the altar, they responded, 'They're four wooden boards, we've nailed them together and we've pulled them apart' " (71). The miners of *Germinal* cannot respond the same way when they confront the bourgeoisie's fetishized objects. That the proletariat as well as the Third Estate has made and can unmake what oppresses it is a supposition, not an experience.

Despite collective memory that it is in no sense absolute, the power of hegemonic conventions during the Restoration was immense. Balzac represented both the positive and negative impact of that power in *Sarrasine* and *Le Père Goriot*, and the being created by Julien Sorel's blue suit is only one of the ways social customs create a daunting reality in *Le Rouge et le noir*. Unlike Balzac and Stendhal's characters, Zola's miners are forced to perform their selfhood in unalleviated opposition to the beliefs organizing their world. They are in the position of the bourgeois delegates to the Estates General prior to annihilation of the Old Regime, and the failure of the workers' revolution that they attempt confines them in a world where their struggle is readily equated with the discourse of the insane. In the words of the bourgeois Deneulin, "We've got nothing to say to them, what do you expect? They don't know any more, all we can do is slaughter them" (1449). What the miners no longer know at the time of revolt, which prompted Deneulin's remarks, are the constitutive principles of bourgeois society. What they cannot yet know are the principles that would organize a different society and a different way to speak what is in it. Deneulin's "we've got nothing to say to them" is perfectly correct but absolutely dependent on the conventions that determine what the verb *say* can meaningfully include among its permissible direct objects. There is nothing to be said to strikers in rebellion because the rules for saying things are inseparable from the socioeconomic subordination under attack. Like the Third Estate in the French Revolution, the proletarian rebels of *Germinal* reject what society needs them to be. Unlike the Third Estate, they fall tragically short of converting society to what they need it to be.

The analogies between the striking workers in *Germinal* and the rebellious bourgeois in the Estates General invite expansion. From the perspective of Austin's ultimate assimilation of performative and constative speech, the power of the king's word in 1789 and the strength of naturalist discourse in Zola's text are directly comparable. Each claims to represent reality as given, and each is shown to depend on reality as interpreted. In the period between June of 1789 and dissolution of the monarchy in 1792, royal authority was in continual flux as revolutionaries defined or diminished the things that the royal word could do. The final decision that it could do nothing came only after agonizing liberation from a world in which it could do everything. The indomitable thrust of Zola's naturalist style makes the same claim to all-inclusive jurisdiction as the king's decrees. Episodes such as that in which the world circumscribed by naturalist description "disappears" consequently have the capital thematic function of indicating how ways of writing interact with ways of acting. In common with Louis XVI, the narrative voice of *Germinal* commands a referential language subject to instant revocation of its referentiality.

The distinction is of course that the French Revolution silenced Louis XVI altogether whereas the naturalist style of *Germinal* always recaptures the prominence Lukács deplored. The tradition of Marxist criticism associated with Lukács is fully justified when it classifies that naturalist style as the implicit appeal for a frozen society in which the ideological law of conservation of hierarchy is no less immutable than the physical law of conservation of matter. My argument with Lukács is not how he interprets Zola's descriptive practice but that he fails to interpret the textual correlation betwen descriptive practice and social vision. When, as in the miners' visit to Hennebeau, social vision becomes troubled, the form of description is altered as well. The overwhelming dominance of naturalist reification in *Germinal* must be analyzed in the context of those moments, however rare, when reification is impossible because the world of fetishized objects has "disappeared."

The novel's title, *Germinal,* makes a strong appeal for reader response to the social ground for whatever connection the text establishes between a name and a thing. Because it is a component of the revolutionary calendar, "Germinal" begins Zola's text with the reminder that every naming operation requires collective ratification, that no description can be objective because every description is a performance. Consider the difference between the month of Germinal and the month of April. The latter figures in a frozen series of signs suggesting that tomorrow will be only yesterday's reproduction; the former proclaims that yesterday's signs are fragile products that tomorrow can easily blow away. For Voloshinov, signs accepted by an established ideology always attempt to disguise the truth of the past as the truth of the present. As the opening speech act of his novel, Zola chose a word specifying that every truth is a temporally specific convention in which yesterday counts only to the extent a collectivity reenacts it today.

To appreciate the thematic impact of the novel's definitive name, compare it to the other titles Zola considered. "Le Grain qui germe" and "Le Sang qui germe" (the germinating seed and the germinating blood), for instance, identify the subject of the narrative to follow as a natural process without connection to human action. "Germinal" specifies that all natural processes are subject to absorption by a social dynamic inaugurated and sustained by human agency. The rickety human structures in "La Maison qui craque" and "Château branlant," the natural catastrophes in "Le Sol qui brûle," "Moisson rouge," and "La Lézarde" all convey the sense of an end to the old without invoking the possibility of a beginning for the new. "Germinal" accepts this possibility as the ineluctable precondition for its own lexical existence.

In other terms, "Germinal" does to the novel as a whole what proletarian self-performance does to Hennebeau's furniture: it historicizes and socializes what would otherwise appear a natural given, makes vulnerable to revolutionary obliteration what would otherwise appear a constant, eternal truth. By the period of the year that it designates—spring—"Germinal" invokes one of the most powerful of humanity's manifold demonstrations that time is cyclical. Yet the very form of the designation insists that the cyclical can become historical, that time can be made the linear production of a future that does something other than repeat the past. The ideological message of the referent clashes with the ideological message of the name, and the novel restages the conflict at every moment of its characters' struggle for their world. An inaugural allusion to successful bourgeois rebellion makes the political stakes of this narrative of unsuccessful proletarian rebellion far weightier than the outcome alone could suggest. Although the bourgeoisie wins the war, the name given the war's annals specifies that victory is due not to the order of the world but only to the varying strength of the belligerents.

The opposition between nature and history enacted by the referent and form of "Germinal" presents significant affinities with the opposition between constative and objective reality enacted by the vagaries of naturalist description. Like the referent in its carapace, nature is an immutable given. Like the constative in its creators' world, history is a human production that must be endlessly renewed or repealed. The nature/history and constative/referential contrasts take ideological punch from the fact that every dominant class must seek to represent the social system that assures its domination as the consequence of conditions no more subject to revision than one season succeeding another or one thing being named by one word. An essential task of ideology is to confuse nature and history until the difference between them is erased from collective consciousness and the conventional effects of conventional procedures appear to be the material effects of a physical cause.

Since the 1960s, the exciting body of French scholarship called sociocriticism has focused highly productive attention on the ideological message conveyed by the myths of nature so important to Zola's compositional strategy. In blunt terms, those myths accomplish nothing less than a textual negation of history. In their own way, they preclude change as stridently as descriptive reification of humanity and its possessions. Along with the spectacular series of images they generate, the natural myths of *Germinal* express reactionary messages that contest all textual moves toward representation of human existence in historical time.

As an example of the analytic value of sociocritical concern with nature's infiltration of society in Zola, let us consider Henri Mitterand's important article "L'Idéologie du mythe dans *Germinal*." For Mitterand, *Germinal*'s allusions to a certain moment of capitalist development are repeatedly displaced by the power of mythic allusions. "Each denoted detail is, if I may say so, impure, weighed down by its absorption of connoted correspondences . . . concrete reality and rational analysis are progressively evacuated to make way for the fantastic and the fabulous" (85; my translation). When the text designates the situation confronting French miners at the end of the nineteenth century, the effect is not verbal mimesis of the real but symbolic domestication of the working class, separated from the bourgeoisie by a barrier as permanent as that between night and day, subterranean mine and open sky. "Social structure is thus, in the textual universe, organically correlated with material structures (light and darkness, above and below ground) and with biological structures. Separation of the two classes is in the order of the natural and eternal, not of the social and transitory. It is a fact of nature, not of culture" (87). Naturalization of the historical guarantees social order in the same way that myths themselves guarantee natural order. Through the tireless operation of what Mitterand calls a "mythifying disguise" (89), *Germinal* conveys the sensation that human society is in its essence organized by the class divisions of nineteenth-century Europe.

Extended and deepened by many of Mitterand's other studies and by such influential articles as Claude Duchet's "Le Trou des bouches noires," the political reading stated in "L'Idéologie du mythe dans *Germinal*" has become a prominent interpretation of the novel's ideological content. There is little serious dissent over the contention that the novel establishes a systematic parallel between a historical socioeconomic system and an ahistorical symbolic order. For some of the most perceptive readers of *Germinal*, the novel's acceptance of a natural paradigm condemns its proletarian characters to a future that will repeat their brutal past.

Yet the syntagmatic axis of this natural paradigm begins with a title announcing that even Nature is historically determined. Whereas Nature admits no revolutions, "Germinal" denotes Nature through a signifier that evokes revolution in the fundamental hermeneutic process of acquiring a signified. Barthes's *Mythologies* defines myth as a depoliticized speech intended to ground a history in Nature, a contingency in eternity (229). The depoliticized discourse of springtime renewal is a perfect example, and it is just this discourse that "Germinal" refutes by transmuting the cyclical into the linear, Nature into history. As introduction to his novel, Zola took a word that contests every naturalizing myth to follow.

According to Mitterand, the textual system of *Germinal* is structured so as to effect a metaphorization of revolt. By representing workers as a force of Nature, the novel's imagery contributes mightily to setting strict limits on human action. Metaphorization and naturalization reinforce one another in a process Mitterand summarizes in this way: "The historical and social denotation is submerged and overwhelmed by the biological and natural connotation" (89). The title *Germinal* reverses this process by conveying a natural and biological signified through a social and historical signifier, reminding the reader that the process of signification is a struggle for power rather than recognition of a fact. The only route to the text is across a word that, instead of metaphorizing revolt, revolutionizes metaphor.

In his history of the French Revolution, Michelet cites the memorable sentence that C.-G. Romme chose to present the republican calendar to the Convention: "Time is at last opening a book to history" (II, 632). Humanity seizes Nature in a series of signs that entwine revolution in temporal notation of every kind. By choosing a component of that sign series to name his narrative of another kind of revolution, Zola continued Romme's project. He too opened his book to history, by using history to open his book.

Readers and critics of *Germinal* agree that the novel's final chapter, especially its final paragraph, furnishes the most compelling illustration of its title. In these famous lines, the social signified and the biological signified interpenetrate in a studied, determined refusal to let either stand apart from the other. Yet the biological signified of springtime concludes a text that begins by submitting springtime to historical transformation. The natural processes finally submerging social strife are first spoken in a word invented by social strife.

It is nevertheless necessary to ask why, if Zola's title subordinates Nature to history, the hierarchy is reversed in the final chapter's indefatigable iteration of such resolutely ahistorical terms as "April" or "germination," both of which take on the referent of "Germinal" but abandon its historicization. If the Nature/history relation is not the same in the month of April as in the month of Germinal, why does *Germinal* conclude in the month of April, when the avenging army of workers seems about to sprout from the earth rather than to organize itself in specific historical circumstances? Does the end of *Germinal* effectively defuse the problematization of Nature in its title?

From a speech-act perspective, the answer is yes. But the same perspective defines any such resolution as a performance that depends on socioeconomic conventions for its capacity to conceal socioeconomic conditions. The novel's title and conclusion express irreconcilable visions of human potential for change. Germinal opens the text, April closes it; April is what Nature grants and promises to repeat for all eternity, Germinal what history produces to free us from all eternity. Conflicting representations of one of time's units make opposite statements about time itself. In Bakhtinian terms, April and Germinal are in a dialogic relationship. Each opposes the other but does not silence it.

And the same dialogic structure of opposition without annihilation permeates all the novel's other nominative oppositions, from the objects inflating naturalist rhetoric to the miners struggling for rhetorical presence. Like the month with two names, the working class is also a single referent with unreconciled representations. In one of their forms, the miners are motionless. Metaphorization of their revolt and naturalization of their world condemn them to paralysis. Collective action changes nothing. Because workers remain after rebellion exactly what they were before it, the words that describe them at the end of the novel are a tragic reworking of the words that introduced them four hundred pages earlier.

Et, du village éteint au Voreux qui soufflait, c'était sous les rafales un lent défilé d'ombres, le départ des charbonniers pour le travail, roulant des épaules, embarrassés de leurs bras, qu'ils croisaient sur la poitrine; tandis que, derrière, le briquet faisait à chacun une bosse. Vêtus de toile mince, ils grelottaient de froid, sans se hâter davantage, débandés le long de la route, avec un piétinement de troupeau.

And, from the darkened village to the roaring Voreux, there was in the gusting winds a slow parade of shadows, the miners setting off for work, rounding their shoulders, awkwardly crossing their arms on their chests; while the food stuck behind them made each one look like a hunchback. Dressed in thin fabric, they were shivering from the cold but still did not hurry, stretched out along the road, tramping like a herd of animals. [1151]

Le troupeau piétinait, des files d'hommes trottant le nez vers la terre, ainsi que du bétail mené à l'abattoir. Ils grelottaient sous leurs minces vêtements de toile, ils croisaient les bras, roulaient les reins, gonflaient le dos, que le briquet, logé entre la chemise et la veste, rendait bossu.

The herd was tramping, lines of men moving with their noses to the ground, like animals led to the slaughterhouse. They were shivering under the thin fabric of their clothes, their backs were round and taut, and the food between their shirt and jacket made them look like hunchbacks. [1582]

The only revolutionary content of these two descriptions comes from the fact that "revolution" also means "repetition." What is the effect of workers' militant solidarity in struggle against the capitalist world? "A slow parade of shadows" becomes "animals led to the slaughterhouse."

Yet this textual stasis must take the measure of a contradictory articulation, that developed by Etienne throughout the novel and given ultimate form in the stirring sense of historical possibilities that punctuate the final chapter to remind us that the defeated army is still a mobilized mass "in a dull rage from the need to continue the struggle" (1582). Those who no longer dare talk have nonetheless managed to redefine their silence. "Thus their defeat reassured nobody, the Montsou bourgeois ... would look over their shoulders to see if their end was coming despite everything, inevitably, there in that great silence. They understood that the revolution would be ceaselessly reborn" (1590). Germinal the month is April plus the French Revolution. *Germinal* the novel is a naturalizing ideology plus intense evocation of proletarian revolution. For workers as for springtime, the validity of a name comes from the efficacity of an act.

In one of his invaluable letters to Van Santen Kolff, Zola described how "Germinal" forced itself on him as the word best constituted to convey the essence of his novel.

And so one day, by accident, the word "Germinal" came to my lips. I didn't want it at first, I found it too mystical, too symbolic, but it represented what I was looking for, a revolutionary April, decrepit society flying away in the springtime. And, little by little, I got used to it, so much so that I couldn't come up with anything else. If it's still obscure for some readers, it's now for me like a burst of sunlight that illuminates the whole work (*il est devenu pour moi comme un coup de soleil qui éclaire toute l'oeuvre*). [Quoted in *Les Rougon-Macquart*, III, 1881].

I take this universal illumination to be the effect of a common polyphony. Neither "Germinal" nor *Germinal* admits univocal interpretation. The word refers to nature but historicizes its sense; in Zola's letter both *April* and *springtime* take the unfamiliar attributes of a revolutionary transformation of society. Analogously, the novel inscribes the bourgeois universe as natural but specifies that this inscription is itself a political act. At the end of the novel as at its beginning, workers are a flock of animals trudging toward a future without hope. Yet they have also become something else, an oppressed class growing conscious that its oppression need not go on forever. The spring morning that concludes *Germinal* conveys the same ideological message as the winter night that opens it, the fatalistic vision of humanity absorbed by an unchangeable absolute. But such a message betrays its own purpose by accepting juxtaposition with a voice that depends for its expressiveness on a world where there are no unchangeable absolutes.

A certain temporal referent is called both April and Germinal. A certain social referent is called both the destruction and the salvation of the world. The "burst of sunlight that illuminates the whole work" is recognition that the relative value of the elements in each of these pairs of names is unstable. During a past revolution, Germinal annihilated April. During "a coming revolution, the real one, the workers' revolution" (1589), the world's salvation will redeem the destruction necessary for revolutionary change. The novel's title announces that its text makes truth a historical conjuncture and the power to speak truth a social conquest.

There are thus two major reasons for reading *Germinal*'s final chapter as the defense and illustration of its title. Besides lyrically combining earth's renewal and workers' revolt, the conclusion

makes this metaphoric combination an overtly political stratagem. For Bakhtin/Voloshinov, every speech act is the response
to another, and any response is engaged in the dynamics of
social conflict. The ability to conceal conflict and present language as the direct, disengaged expression of reality is the ultimate ideological mystification. *Germinal's* last chapter
problematizes such mystification by alternating mutually contradictory languages, that of a rising sun and that of a rising
class. As a consequence, each language assumes an obvious place
in the struggle for meaning at the core of Bakhtinian dialogism.
The free indirect discourse associated with Etienne pokes holes
in narrative rhetoric to manifest narration's ideological purpose.
The warm morning of April's eternal return comes up against
the hot morning of historical change, "the morning they'd all
stand side by side, when there would be millions of workers"
(1590). Novelistic description gives itself a context that defines
it as a voice assigned the mission of eliminating another voice,
as the vision against which the miners must perform themselves.

The socialized dialogue concluding *Germinal* furnishes a
point-by-point contrast to the monologue that opens it. In the
first chapter, Nature unrelentingly strives to silence workers,
and the text serves as Nature's accomplice. "A gust of wind
made it impossible to talk. . . . Their voices were lost, rushing
winds carried their words away in a melancholy screech" (1135–
36). Shoulder to shoulder with these natural interruptions of
workers' direct discourse stands the text's refusal to accord them
an indirect discourse worth attention. Blown away by the wind
and hidden away by the narrative, workers' voices articulate
nothing at the beginning of *Germinal*. In stark contrast, at the
novel's end those voices make themselves heard in an extraordinary performative crescendo. The novel that opens on one
voice alone closes by accepting the basic dialogic principle of
the equal value of contradictory voices in antagonistic
confrontation.

The first chapter takes Etienne as its point of view solely in
the physical sense of point of view. The worker is not a consciousness but a camera, and there are compelling reasons why
"his empty worker's head" (1133) is among the most quoted

features of the first chapter's Etienne. The empty head is apparent in absolute intellectual and emotional passivity with systematically dehumanizing effect. It would be legitimate to argue that the first pages of *Germinal* go so far as to deny Etienne the power to perceive as well as the power to think. Although the novel's second sentence defines its protagonist as the center of description, what is described is not what Etienne sees but what is beyond his view: "Before him, he did not even see the black ground, and he had the sensation of the vast flat surroundings only because of the gusting March wind" (1133). In a striking reversal of standard third-person narration, the verbs *see* and *have the sensation* acquire their standard objects only after their negation has excised the third-person observer. Like Hennebeau's furniture, the earth and sky possess autonomous textual presence that transcends workers' faculties.

When the worker's empty head has something in it, the subject of his thought is his failure to live like a human being: "Il songeait à lui, à son existence de vagabond, depuis huit jours qu'il cherchait une place; il se revoyait dans son atelier du chemin de fer, giflant son chef, chassé de Lille, chassé de partout" (He was thinking of himself, of his vagabond existence in the week he had been looking for a job; he saw himself in the railroad yard, hitting his foreman, driven out of Lille, driven out of everywhere, 1135). Compare the thought of the same worker, once more without a job and without a home, in the final chapter. "Il songeait à lui, il se sentait fort, mûri par sa dure expérience au fond de la mine" (He was thinking of himself, he felt strong, ripened by his hard experience down in the mine, 1588). Again *Germinal*'s conclusion repeats its beginning, and again the repeated words do different things. In the first chapter, a worker's rebellion produced an empty head, an enfeebled body, and a stifled voice. In the last chapter, that same worker's rebellion has produced a committed socialist, sure of his bodily strength and endowed with a voice inscribed as the equal of omniscient narration. Where there was an empty head there is a full presence. Where there was a terroristic monologue there is authentic dialogism.

What Voloshinov calls the "*inner dialectic quality* of the sign

[that] comes out fully in the open only in times of social crises or revolutionary changes" is at last fully in the open in Zola's narrative of a social crisis without revolutionary change. What could be more straightforward than to call April April? Nothing at all, except in a text proclaiming that the value of this simple name shifts with history: in another period, April is Germinal. What could be more logical than to compare a mass threatening the order of society to a cosmic catastrophe overturning the order of Nature? Nothing at all, except in a text that represents the threat from the perspective of the mass as well as from the perspective of its rulers. Voloshinov's "uniaccentual" signs do not mystify when continually interrupted by signs with a different accent and a different message. On one hand, the final chapter exalts bursting seeds and universal love, "le bruit des germes [qui] s'épandait en un grand baiser" (1591); on the other, it envisions "a coming revolution, the real one, the workers' revolution." Such contrastingly accented language accumulates until the class origins of a paean to Nature resound as clearly as those of a call to arms.

The thesis that *Germinal* incorporates the multiple accents essential to dialogic composition seems to me the only way to explain the stunning dialogism that has characterized all political readings of the novel since its publication. Few literary works have elicited more contradictory ideological interpretations. For Angus Wilson a "personally felt and imagined illustration of the 1848 Communist Manifesto" (116), *Germinal* is for René Ternois the reactionary vision of a working class condemned to oscillate forever between sheepish docility and wolfish destruction: "Nothing in this book allows us to think that the people will one day have a clearer awareness of what they can be, of what they can create" (60; my translation). In an allusion to Paule Lejeune's *Germinal: Un Roman antipeuple*, some critics have divided Zola's readers into those who would endorse such a subtitle and those who find instead a *roman peuple* in this story of aborted revolt.

For an example of this dichotomy, take David Baguley's "*Germinal: Une moisson de texte*," which examines "a series of scenes that are all oriented around a single theme: the miners' linguistic impotence and their submission to bourgeois discourse" (393; my translation). As the prodigiously informed bibliographer of Zola studies from the nineteenth century to the present, Baguley is well aware that his thesis of the miners' linguistic impotence must construct itself against the critical tradition that reads *Germinal* as the narrative of workers coming to language for the first time. His article is consequently in open dialogue with that tradition, and I quote Baguley quoting one of his interlocutors. "It is therefore important to qualify if not reject the remark of the American critic Irving Howe, according to which '*Germinal* begins one of the central myths of the modern era: the story of the mute learning to speak' " (394). A single novel orients itself around workers' linguistic impotence and makes itself the narrative of their language acquisition. The contradiction is pointed and direct, and Baguley's bibliographies are the record of an unbroken process of analogous affirmations and denials. Political interpretations of *Germinal* are a series of assertions that endlessly contradict one another.

And the core of dialogism is also a series of assertions that endlessly contradict one another. From a Bakhtinian perspective, every unitary interpretation of *Germinal* elicits its own refutation because the novel itself refutes all the political points it makes. The abundance of textual evidence for a progressive vision is matched by that of the evidence for a reactionary vision, and perhaps the most fascinating component of the radical transformation of critical methodologies applied to Zola since the early 1960s is that contemporary critics are no more agreed on the political sense of *Germinal* than were Wilson and Ternois. In its intensity, the controversy over *Germinal*'s political meaning furnishes strong documentary evidence that this text defines all its messages as contradictory products of an oppositional structure. Both an illustration of the *Communist Manifesto* and a *roman antipeuple*, *Germinal* announces that literature is no more suited for "natural" interpretation than any other human creation. By its refusal to admit a uniaccentual reading without immediately provoking that reading's contradiction, *Germinal* finally undermines uniaccentual thought itself. The realist constative wholly supplants the naturalist referent.

The textual components of Zola's novel that have figured most prominently in critical discussion of its political stance almost all present a matrix identifying them as the expression of one among many social visions, as the utterance of an interlocutor engaged in historical dialogue. Consider the march of miners in revolt before the bourgeois in hiding, so celebrated a passage that I will quote only those sections that have been the object of especially important commentary.

Les femmes avaient paru, près d'un millier de femmes, aux cheveux épars, dépeignées par la course, aux guenilles montrant la peau nue, des nudités de femelles lasses d'enfanter des meurt-de-faim.... Et les hommes déboulèrent ensuite, deux mille furieux.... Les yeux brûlaient, on voyait seulement les trous des bouches noires.... C'était la vision rouge de la révolution qui les emporteraient tous, fatalement, par une soirée sanglante de cette fin de siècle. Oui, un soir, le peuple lâché, débridé, galoperait ainsi sur les chemins; et il ruissellerait du sang des bourgeois, il promènerait des têtes, il sèmerait l'or des coffres éventrés. Les femmes hurleraient, les hommes auraient ces mâchoires de loups, ouvertes pour mordre.

The women had appeared, nearly a thousand women, their hair wild, disheveled by their march, their rags showing bare skin, the nakedness of she-creatures tired of giving birth to children who starve.... And then the men rushed into view, two thousand maniacs.... Their eyes were fiery, only the black holes of their mouths could be seen.... It was the red vision of the revolution that would inevitably carry them all away one bloody evening as this century came to its end. Yes, one night the people, unbridled, unleashed, would gallop down the road like this, and bourgeois blood would flow, heads would be on pikes, gold would pour from gutted coffers. Women would be screaming, men would have those wolf mouths, open and ready to bite. [1435–37]

Stylistic bestialization of the proletariat reaches a blatant extreme here. Women are "femelles," men wolves, and each sex roars instead of speaking, gallops instead of walking. The threat mounted by such creatures is not social change but unchecked savagery. *Après nous la ménagerie.*

Yet *Germinal*—as if to illustrate the dialogic principle that it is not experience that determines expression but expression that organizes experience—encloses this celebrated passage in two separate statements that bestialization of workers is being performed by bourgeois conventions. Punctuated throughout by the direct evaluation of the bourgeois Négrel and the women with him, this "red vision of revolution" is no less an instance of free indirect discourse than Etienne's green vision of revolution in the novel's final chapter. Description of the miners' march begins with the information that Lucie and Jeanne Deneulin, hidden in a stable, "had put their eye against a crack, eager not to miss any of the spectacle" (1435). The following pages are the spectacle of a spectacle. The reader sees not the miners but a bourgeois seeing of the miners, not reality but its explicitly ideological deformation. One class's catastrophe becomes destruction of the world because it is contemplated by the threatened class. Rather than the end of civilization, the apocalyptic style announces the end of one form of society as imagined by those whose lives depend on its perpetuation.

To emphasize that the red vision of revolution is only one of its possible colors, *Germinal* puts the apocalypse in the middle of a chapter that begins and ends with a remarkable demonstration of how bourgeois existence affects workers' representation. Just before the miners' march, Hennebeau learns of his wife's most recent infidelity. Just after it, his despair provokes an extraordinary libidinal fantasy leading him to see workers on strike as animals in heat. This textual organization is not surprising if we understand both bourgeois visions of the miners as a reiterated demonstration that observed reality is consubstantial with an observing ideology. Hennebeau's sexual hysteria is expressed in direct discourse, the political hysteria of other bourgeois characters in indirect discourse. But their amalgamation in a single chapter unites them in a cogent textual display of the impossibility of separating any class's vision of the world from the world constituting it as a class.

This impossibility is of course central to the dialogic organization of *Germinal*. Even when reifying discourse appears to emanate from a neutral, objective space, its context identifies it as the product of a politicized space. *Germinal* confronts not accurate and deformed visions but different conventions for determining accuracy. When the narrative voice explicitly contests workers' hopes, it abandons its claims to omniscience and accepts identification as one performance of truth among others.

Memorable examples of such renunciation recur during the nights of political discussion between Etienne and the Maheu family, the nights when Etienne's passion for change takes the form of moving political eloquence. At several points, the text breaks off the discussions to deny the impression that such eloquence might produce, that of the birth of authentic class consciousness among oppressed workers. Here is one of the most celebrated interruptions: "And, continuously, this dream grew larger and more beautiful, became all the more seductive the higher it rose into the impossible" (1278). Incontestably, the word *impossible* ridicules the vision of social justice that came before it. Expansion and improvement of working-class life suddenly becomes a stupid, dangerous illusion, the sick dream of a disoriented mind.

There is nonetheless a sense in which the very violence of *impossible* prohibits any such monologic understanding of its interpolation. The word is clearly not a judge but one of the antagonists, the strong refusal of a threat to the ideology it expresses. Workers' speech elicits speech against workers. Social struggle is manifest in lexical contradiction, with each pole of the contradiction attached to a position in the struggle. The political function of *impossible* is strident; obviously inserted in a dialogue, this depreciation of the miners in no way invalidates the contradictory discourse that provokes and prepares it. Conflict is not between truth and error but between irreconcilable truths performed by different experiences of the human condition.

"The higher it rose into the impossible" is the final clause of a paragraph that begins with this description of Etienne's vision of another world.

D'une voix ardente, il parlait sans fin. C'était, brusquement, l'horizon fermé qui éclatait, une trouée de lumière dans la vie sombre de ces pauvres gens. L'éternel recommencement de la misère, le travail de brute, ce destin de bétail qui donne sa laine et qu'on égorge, tout le malheur disparaissait, comme balayé par un grand coup de soleil.

In a burning voice he would speak on and on. Suddenly the closed horizon split open, there was a breach of light in the dark life of these poor people. The eternal recurrence of poverty, the labor of a brute, this fate of animals that give their wool before being slaughtered, all the misery disappeared, as if swept away by a great burst of sunlight. [1278]

As the dream of justice is a "breach of light" in the dark life of the poor, so it is a black spot in the radiant existence of the rich. *Impossible* combats that blackness by promising that the endless cycle of poverty is truly an endless cycle.

However, the essence of dialogism is that its assertions can never completely efface their contraries. Instead of refuting the paragraph's opening words, its conclusion continues the dispute they undertake. In the terms of one side in this dispute, the dream of justice is a great burst of sunlight, *un grand coup de soleil* dissipating working-class despair. I contend that this sunburst is the same as the one we have already encountered, the "coup de soleil" invoked when Zola explained the title "Germinal": "If it's still obscure for some readers, it has become for me a burst of sunlight that illuminates the whole work." What Etienne says to the Maheu family is identical to what Zola's title says to his readers, the categorical refutation of every form of monologic language in the name of a signifying practice inseparable from a social situation.

Far more than a coincidence, the image of the sunburst bound to the workers' revolutionary speech and to the revolutionary title of their story expresses a fundamental thematic identity. In both cases, a verbal form alien to dominant discourse takes legitimacy from its appeal to a different historical moment producing different rules for what words can do.

During his conversations in the middle of the novel as during his meditation at its conclusion, Etienne comes up against a narrative presence that contests everything he articulates. But this narrative voice places itself under the aegis of a title aligned with Etienne, with all those who rebel against the uniaccentual representation of reality. Denigrated by the language that denotes them, the miners are justified by the title which claims that language as its own. Their discourse violates the text but accomplishes its name. Let Bakhtin define the result: "In the novel, language does not merely represent; it is itself an object of representation. Novelistic discourse is always self-critical" (quoted in Todorov, 66). The dominant function of the title of *Germinal* is to make the beginning of novelistic discourse the first move in its radical self-criticism.

In his highly influential essay "Ideology and Ideological State Apparatuses," Louis Althusser identifies a referential view of language with a mystified view of human subjectivity. In both cases, what is actually a social construct appears to its constructors as hopelessly beyond their control.

> As St. Paul admirably put it, it is in the "Logos," meaning in ideology, that we "live and move and have our being." It follows that, for you and for me, the category of the subject is a primary "obviousness" (obviousnesses are always primary): it is clear that you and I are subjects (free, ethical, etc. . . .). Like all obviousnesses, including those that make a word "name a thing" or "have a meaning" (therefore including the obviousness of the "transparency" of language), the "obviousness" that you and I are subjects—and that that does not cause any problems—is an ideological effect, the elementary ideological effect. [171–72]

Out of context, that passage reads as more abstruse than it is. The goal of "Ideology and Ideological State Apparatuses" is to confound the vulgar Marxist notion that human existence can be readily understood by separating what is real—the material infrastructure in a given form of production—from the imaginary ideologies that conceal the actual nature of the real from those who live it. For Althusser, this neat separation ignores the fact that ideas are lived, that every subject "must '*act* according to his ideas,' must therefore inscribe his own ideas as a free subject in the actions of his material practice" (168; here as in all subsequent quotations from Althusser, emphasis is in the original). Practice and theory, materiality and ideology, cannot be separated because each produces the other as a condition of perpetuating itself.

Although "ideological state apparatuses," for example educational and religious institutions, are Althusser's principal evidence for ideology's material existence, they are by no means the only way that ideas are manifest in the objective circumstances inclosing those who hold them. Althusser is quite willing to employ rhetorical overkill in insisting, repetitively and emphatically, that ideas become material in the life of an individual as well as in the institutions of a society. "I shall therefore say that, where only a single subject (such and such an individual) is concerned, the existence of the ideas of his belief is material in that *his ideas are his material actions inserted into material practices governed by material rituals*" (169). Reminiscent of Gertrude Stein's rose, Louis Althusser's ideas are material are material are material. Because any subject must act out as well as hold to a belief, it is absurd to posit a dichotomy between belief and life.

The brutal domination of the word *material* in "Ideology and Ideological State Apparatuses" derives from Althusser's acceptance of an implied reader who is convinced that ideology and matter are mutually exclusive. The assumption is that for such a reader materiality itself is unproblematic, and the strategy is consequently to move ideas from the realm of spirit into that of matter: actions, rituals, praxis, state apparatuses. Less heavy-handed but more consequential is Althusser's problematization of the very opposition between matter and spirit. Practices and institutions are the product as well as the materialization of human subjects in their subjectivity, and this subjectivity is the product of ideology.

Althusser's celebrated pronouncement that ideology interpellates individuals as subjects has as its corollary that there can be no human productivity apart from ideological interpellation. Because what humanity does depends absolutely on what it is, the material conditions of existence are in the same mutually constitutive relationship to ideology as is ideology to subjectivity. "I say: the category of the subject is constitutive of all ideology, but at the same time and immediately I add that *the category of the subject is only constitutive of all ideology insofar as all ideology has the function (which defines it) of "constituting" concrete individuals as subjects.* In the interaction of this double constitution exists the functioning of all ideology" (171). Subjectivity is an abstraction, individuals are concrete. Yet the abstract constitutes the concrete no less than the reverse, and another classic Marxist sequence is discombobulated.

The very concept of sequentiality, with the hierarchy it implies, is untenable when each step in a sequence is always already what succeeds it: "Ideology has always-already interpellated individuals as subjects, which amounts to making it clear that individuals are always-already interpellated by ideology as subjects, which necessarily leads us to one last proposition: *individuals are always-already subjects.* Hence individuals are 'abstract' with respect to the subjects they always-already are" (175–76). "Abstract" is in quotations because it can no longer be comfortably distinguished from its binary opposite "concrete." Matter and spirit, concrete things and abstract ideas, are inextricable in Althusser's version of the functioning of ideology. Each is always already the other, each simultaneously constitutes and is constituted by that which is ordinarily its negation. Ideology interpellates individuals as subjects, but those individuals are always already what they become when ideology interpellates them. Althusser's most celebrated contribution to the crucial contemporary debate on ideology posits a process and articulates a category that are both dissolved by the argument in which they figure. There is no such thing as an "individual" in the sense of an undefined person awaiting ideological subjectification, and there can consequently be no temporal component to the interpellation process. As "ideology has no history" (159 and passim), that which ideology does has no past before the doing was done. The concrete is always already abstracted, the abstract always already concretized.

The implications of Althusser's dizzying dissolution of the axiomatic distinctions that ground much traditional social analysis are extensive and profound. The one that is most pertinent here is the material reality of what is ordinarily opposed term by term to the reality of matter, for Althusser's concept of ideology is in many ways analogous to the realist constative. The elementary ideological effect is the "primary obviousness" not only of human subjectivity but also of language's transparency, of that which makes a word name a thing (171–72). Toward all primary obviousnesses, Althusser's stance is of course to show that what appears prior to society is in actuality a social production. But that stance immediately requires demonstrating that the *power* of a primary obviousness is not in the least diminished or dispersed when its supposed *origin* is demystified. The subject produced by ideology performs "*material actions inserted into material practices governed by material rituals,*" and the material performed is no less a primary obviousness than Dr. Johnson's stone, the vulgar Marxist's means of production, or the king of England in Bertrand Russell's "On Denoting."

Althusser's trajectory is thus strikingly similar to Austin's use of *How to Do Things with Words* both to distinguish and to assimilate constative and performative speech. In the Austinian problematic, words that state a truth are different from words that invoke a convention; but at the same time stating a truth is one of the conventions words invoke. Austin's desire to "play Old Harry" (151) with the value-fact fetish leads straight to recognition that facts remain factual even when they are recognized as values in the same way and for the same reasons that Althusser's desire to confound the material/ideological dichotomy leads to anaphoric exaltation of the word *material* as a necessary step in debunking matter's primary obviousness.

For Austin, illocution differs from locution "in that the [illocutionary] act is constituted not by intention or by fact, essentially but by *convention* (which is, of course, a fact)" (128). That which distinguishes illocution from locution is also that which identifies them. Convention is both distinct from and the same thing as fact, and Austin's parenthetical interpolation annihilates a primary obviousness with the same casual mastery as Althusser's problematics of the material.

Like Austin and Althusser, realist fiction conveys a vision of the world in which the deconstruction of facts and matter as something more real than social or ideological productions coexists with spirited defense of those productions as matters of fact. Abolition of a ground is inseparable from preservation of what it supported; refusal of an opposition prepares affirmation of the attributes foregrounded when the opposition is posited. Balzac, Stendhal, and Zola refuse primary obviousnesses with Althusser's firmness and they share Austin's delight in playing Old Harry with facts in themselves. But novelists and theorists also converge in refusing to let their acute perception of ideology's operations induce insensitivity to the consequences that follow those operations' successfully concealed institution. Because what a collectivity understands as a fact remains a fact even though not in itself, the realist project entails deep respect for, as well as relentless exposure of, the reality effect.

Applied to *Germinal*, the Althusserian and Austinian vision of ideology suggests the amalgamation of the nouns that head this chapter's title, *performance* and *class*. The socioeconomic entity called a class is in no sense an objectively constituted group susceptible to accurate and total delineation through correct analysis of who owns the means of production. A class must be a performance if it is to be. The means of production produce nothing if the relations of production come apart, and those relations are the conventional effects of the conventional procedures on which the Austinian performative depends absolutely. Yet once performed, a class's reality is crushing. Exactly like the purely objective facts of ownership, the felicitous institution of a conventional status establishes the reality in which we live and move and have our being. One of the many reasons Althusser's identification of ideology with Paul's logos is so instructive is that *logos* is the West's most widespread shorthand for words that do things indistinguishable from things that are not words. When a collectivity felicitously says "Let there be class," there *is* class.

And when a collectivity says "Let words name a thing," that is what words do. As a consequence, it seems not at all fortuitous that Zola's work distinguishes itself from that of Balzac and Stendhal in two major ways: introduction of working-class protagonists and enhancement of physical description to the point of stupefaction. The body of novels that first gave workers a commanding fictional presence is also the body of novels in which the obviousness that words name a thing became so strident that many readers concluded that words could do nothing else. Lanson and Lukács approach Zola from incompatible starting points and arrive at an identical conclusion because Zola made some such conclusion impossible to miss. The transparency of language is almost axiomatic when language resolutely declines every function other than directing attention to its referents.

Analogously, the naturalness of class divisions is unquestionable when they are performed with such consistency that they delineate permanent ways of being. Ideology acted out as *"material actions inserted into material practices governed by material rituals"* becomes for its actors precisely what Zola's style is for Lanson, something as heavy and powerful as matter, something that for all practical purposes is in fact matter. Althusser's concept of ideology carefully distinguishes between the real and the imaginary while also asserting that it is only through the imaginary that the real is experienced: "The representation given to individuals of their (individual) relation to the social relations which govern their conditions of existence and their collective and individual life [is] necessarily an imaginary relation" (165). When the real is of necessity represented through the imaginary, the imaginary has its own reality. Zola's workers represent themselves through forms that assume the density of naturalist description at its most cumbersome. Their subservience is their reality as the language of their novel is, obviously, a transparent opening to the things it names.

A principal theme of the preceding discussion of *Germinal* was consequently the simultaneity of workers' refusal of subservience and textual refusal to annotate things as autonomous. Both primary obviousnesses, that of language's referentiality and that of workers' subjectification as subservient, abandon their credibility at the same time. When an imaginary relation to reality is no longer performed through material actions and material practices, matter becomes imaginary in the traditional sense of the imagination. Like Althusser's vision of subjectivity and ideology, *Germinal*'s representation of working-class docility and matter's ontology are mutually constitutive. Each always already is, except when the other is not. Each has no history except when history transforms the other into something it was not yet.

In *Germinal*, there is a despairingly transitory character to the moments class is performed in a manner different from what is always already prescribed, when reality is represented as something other than what is always already there. *Germinal* narrates not a revolution but a revolt, and textual suggestions of revolutionary change always segue into textual affirmations that no change shall occur. In Zola's novel, Althusser's refusal to admit a comforting opposition between matter and ideology appears as a parallel between ideological inertia and material presence. Social challenges to what is provoke textual interrogation of the meaning of *is*, but neither the challenge nor the interrogation sustains itself. The novel performs class and matter with the same skill after undermining its own performance as before.

Here is Karl Marx on the material force of ideology: "Men make their own history, but they do not make it just as they please; they do not make it under circumstances chosen by themselves, but under circumstances directly encountered, given and transmitted from the past. The tradition of all the dead generations weighs like a nightmare on the brain of the living" (15). As Althusser's ideas are practiced, so Marx's tradition has weight. In both thinkers as in *Germinal*, the insight that constative reality is a human performance does not in the least attenuate reality's overriding impact on human existence. The nightmare on the brain of the striking workers in Germinal correlates directly with textual solidity of the universe not chosen by themselves.

The previous argument that this universe is in a dialogic relationship with a world that has yet to be created relied heavily on the choice of the word *germinal* to introduce fictional representation of the nightmare. This book therefore concludes where it began, with the French Revolution's object lesson for the world on the connections between sociopolitical change and the collectively perceived validity of verbal representation as inherited from the past. The weight of all the dead generations is a palpable component of the experience of reading *Germinal*, yet the possibilities that are accorded to generations to come permit the novel to suggest that the weight can be thrown off and forgotten. According to Marx, humanity must produce its history in a world it did not make; the variegated force of descriptive discourse in *Germinal* is an extraordinary demonstration of fiction's ability to show the world not made and to expose its susceptibility to being unmade.

This book therefore also concludes on the other topic with which it began, the dual ontology of constative reality as defined by J. L. Austin and as represented in French realist fiction. Conventional production of truth institutes facts that are both overwhelming and subject to instant collapse, and each of the foregoing chapters has sought to demonstrate realist representation of the facts instituted as no less tenacious than tenuous, as no more permanent than transitory. The realist constative names an absence and a presence, a fullness and an emptiness, what is most abstract and what is most concrete. To end on Althusser is to suggest that this duality is operative in the conflicts that transform the world most decisively as well as in the literature that represents the world most convincingly.

Works Cited

Althusser, Louis. *Lenin and Philosophy.* Trans. Ben Brewster. New York: Monthly Review, 1971.

Auerbach, Erich. *Mimesis.* Trans. Willard R. Trask. Princeton: Princeton University Press, 1953.

Austin, J. L. *How to Do Things with Words.* Cambridge: Harvard University Press, 1975.

Baguley, David. *Bibliographie de la critique sur Emile Zola.* 2 vols. Toronto: Toronto University Press, 1976, 1982.

—— "*Germinal:* Une moisson de texte." *Revue d'histoire littéraire de la France* (May–June 1985), 389–400.

de Balzac, Honoré. *Le Contrat de mariage.* In *La Comédie humaine.* 12 vols. Paris: Pléiade, 1976. 3:527–653.

—— *Illusions perdues.* In *La Comédie humaine.* 5:109–732.

—— *Le Père Goriot.* Paris: Garnier, 1961.

—— *Sarrasine.* In Roland Barthes, *S/Z.* Paris: Seuil, 1970.

Barthes, Roland. "The Death of the Author." *Image Music Text.* Trans. Stephen Heath. New York: Hill & Wang, 1977.

—— "Le Discours de l'histoire." *Social Science Information* 7, 4 (1967), 65–75.

—— "L'Effet de réel." *Communications* 11 (1968), 84–89.

—— *Mythologies.* Paris: Seuil, 1957.

—— *S/Z.* Paris: Seuil, 1970.

Beckett, Samuel. *Three Novels.* New York: Grove, 1965.

de Bonald, Louis-Gabriel-Amboise. *Oeuvres.* 12 vols. Paris: Adrien Le Clère, 1817–26.

Brunot, Ferdinand. *Histoire de la langue française.* 13 vols. Paris: Colin, 1905–69.

Buchez, P.-J.-B., and P. C. Roux. *Histoire parlementaire de la révolution française.* 40 vols. Paris: Paulin, 1834–38.

Works Cited

Carroll, David. "Mimesis Reconsidered." *Diacritics* 5 (Summer 1975), 5–12.

de Chateaubriand, François-René. *Mémoires d'outre-tombe*. 4 vols. Paris: Flammarion, 1948.

de Man, Paul. *Allegories of Reading*. New Haven: Yale University Press, 1979.

Derrida, Jacques. *La Carte postale*. Paris: Flammarion, 1980.

—— *Otobiographies*. Paris: Galilée, 1984.

—— "Signature Event Context." In *Margins of Philosophy*. Trans. Alan Bass. Chicago: University of Chicago Press, 1982. Pp. 309–30.

Duchet, Claude. "Le Trou des bouches noires: Parole, société, révolution dans *Germinal*." *Littérature* 24 (1976), 11–39.

Eagleton, Terry. "Wittgenstein's Friends." In *Against the Grain*. London: Verso, 1986. Pp. 99–130.

Felman, Shoshana. *The Literary Speech Act*. Trans. Catherine Porter. Ithaca: Cornell University Press, 1983.

Fish, Stanley. *Is There a Text in This Class?* Cambridge: Harvard University Press, 1980.

—— "With the Compliments of the Author: Reflections on Austin and Derrida." *Critical Inquiry* 8 (Summer 1982), 693–721.

Furet, François. *Penser la révolution française*. Paris: Gallimard, 1978.

Furet, François, and Denis Richet. *La Révolution*. 2 vols. Paris: Hachette, 1965.

Genette, Gérard. *Figures II*. Paris: Seuil, 1968.

Gontaut-Biron, Marie. *Mémoires*. Paris: Plon, 1893.

Höfner, Eckhard. *Literarität und Realität*. Heidelberg: Carl Winter, 1980.

Jakobson, Roman. "Linguistics and Poetics." In *Selected Writings*. 7 vols. The Hague: Mouton, 1981. 3:18–51.

—— "On Realism in Art." In L. Matejka and K. Pomorska, eds., *Readings in Russian Poetics*. Cambridge: MIT Press, 1971. Pp. 38–46.

Jameson, Fredric. *The Political Unconscious*. Ithaca: Cornell University Press, 1981.

Johnson, Barbara. *The Critical Difference*. Baltimore: Johns Hopkins University Press, 1980.

Lacan, Jacques. *Ecrits: A Selection*. Trans. Alan Sheridan. New York: Norton, 1977.

—— *The Language of the Self*. Trans. Anthony Wilden. New York: Dell, 1968.

Works Cited

Lanson, G., and P. Tuffrau. *Manuel illustré d'histoire de la littérature française*. Paris: Hachette, 1931.

Larousse, Pierre. *Grand Dictionnaire universel du XIXe siècle*. 17 vols. Paris: Larousse, 1866–90.

Lefebvre, Henri. *Au-delà du structuralisme*. Paris: Anthropos. 1971.

Lejeune, Paule. *Germinal: Un roman antipeuple*. Paris: Nizet, 1978.

Lukács, Gyorgy. "Narrate or Describe?" In *Writer and Critic and Other Essays*. Trans. Arthur D. Kahn. New York: Grosset and Dunlap, 1970. Pp. 110–48.

——*Studies in European Realism*. New York: Grosset and Dunlap, 1964.

de Maistre, Joseph. *Du pape*. Paris: Charpentier, n.d.

Martineau, Henri. *L'Œuvre de Stendhal*. Paris: Albin Michel, 1951.

Marx, Karl. *The Eighteenth Brumaire of Louis Bonaparte*. New York: International Publishers, 1964.

Michelet, Jules. *Histoire de la révolution française*. 2 vols. Paris: Pléiade, 1952.

Mitterand, Henri. "L'Idéologie du mythe dans *Germinal*. In Pierre Léon, ed. *Problèmes de l'analyse textuelle*. Montreal: Didier, 1971. Pp. 83–90.

de Musset, Alfred. *Œuvres complètes en prose*. Paris: Pléiade, 1951.

Prendergast, Christopher. *The Order of Mimesis*. Cambridge: Cambridge University Press, 1986.

Russell, Bertrand. "On Denoting." *Mind*, n.s. 14 (1905), 479–93.

de Saussure, Ferdinand. *Cours de linguistique générale*. Paris: Payot, 1955.

Searle, John. "A Classification of Illocutionary Acts." *Language in Society* 5 (April 1976), 1–23.

—— "Reiterating the Differences: A Reply to Derrida." *Glyph*, no. 1 (1977), 198–208.

—— *Speech Acts*. Cambridge: Cambridge University Press, 1969.

Sieyès, Emmanuel Joseph. *Qu'est-ce que le tiers état?* Geneva: Droz, 1970.

de Staël, Germaine. *Considérations sur les principaux événements de la révolution française*. 2 vols. Paris: Delaunay, 1818.

Stendhal. *Le Rouge et le noir*. Paris: Flammarion, 1964.

Ternois, René. *Zola et son temps*. Paris: Les Belles Lettres, 1961.

Todorov, Tzvetan. *Mikhail Bakhtin: The Dialogical Principle*. Trans. Wlad Godzich. Minneapolis: University of Minnesota Press, 1984.

Voloshinov, V. N. *Marxism and the Philosophy of Language*. Trans. L. Matejka and I. R. Titunik. New York: Seminar Press, 1973.

Works Cited

Wilson, Angus. *Emile Zola.* New York: Morrow, 1952.

Wittgenstein, Ludwig. *Philosophical Investigations.* Trans. G. E. M. Anscombe. New York: Macmillan, 1958.

Zola, Emile. *Germinal.* In *Les Rougon-Macquart,* vol. III. Paris: Pléiade, 1965.

Index

Index

Library of Congress Cataloging-in-Publication Data

Petrey, Sandy.
    Realism and revolution : Balzac, Stendhal, Zola, and the
performances of history / Sandy Petrey.
        p.   cm.
    Bibliography: p.
    Includes index.
    ISBN 0-8014-2216-7
        1. French fiction—19th century—History and criticism.
2. Historical fiction, French—History and criticism.   3. Balzac,
Honoré de, 1799–1850—Knowledge—History.   4. Stendhal, 1783–1843—
Knowledge—History.   5. Zola, Émile, 1840–1902—Knowledge—History.
6. Realism in literature.   7. France—History—Revolution,
1789–1799—Literature and the revolution.   I. Title.
PQ653.P48 1989
843'.7'0912—dc19   88-18117